Paper to Practice:
Using the TESOL English Language Proficiency Standards in PreK–12 Classrooms

 TESOL Teachers of English to Speakers of Other Languages, Inc.

Typeset in Berkeley and News Gothic
by Capitol Communications Systems, Inc., Crofton, Maryland USA
Printed by United Graphics Incorporated, Mattoon, Illinois USA

Teachers of English to Speakers of Other Languages, Inc.
700 South Washington Street, Suite 200
Alexandria, Virginia 22314 USA
Tel. 703-836-0774 • Fax 703-836-6447 • E-mail info@tesol.org • http://www.tesol.org/

Publishing Manager: Carol Edwards
Copy Editor: Rebecca Rauff
Additional Reader: Kelly Graham
Cover Design: Amanda VanStaalduinen

ISBN 9781931185554
Library of Congress Control Number 2009900288.

Contents

List of Figures

ৡেন্ত

Acknowledgments

This project has been labor intensive. We have conceptualized and reconceptualized how to present the information in this book so that it is meaningful to all educators working with English language learners, irrespective of where they are located, what policies are in place, how they may teach, and what resources are available. Lynore Carnuccio has helped us through this thinking process and has contributed by providing a teacher's perspective. We thank her for her time, her help in the organization of the book, and her expertise in teacher education.

The development of the TESOL English language proficiency standards matrix, along with the adaptable usage of its components and elements, has been influenced by the work of the World-Class Instructional Design and Assessment (WIDA) Consortium. We acknowledge the valuable role of the consortium in advancing the instruction and assessment of English language learners in elementary and secondary settings.

To keep our attention focused on practice, Michele Mason has shared her classroom teacher experience—as have students in our education classes and participants in our workshops. David Slavit has checked and confirmed the authenticity of the content-based information in the book. Along the way, the manuscript has been reviewed and revised multiple times. Members of the TESOL Standards Committee and the TESOL Book Publications Committee have provided valuable feedback and comments. Ann Snow, liaison to the English language proficiency standards team, has given us encouragement and sage advice whenever asked.

TESOL Central Office has given a helpful hand and a gentle push to ensure an exemplary product. Over the past 3 years, John Segota has arranged many a conference call and meeting. He has advocated on our behalf in communicating with TESOL staff and committee chairs. Carol Edwards has been a wonderful listener and has dedicated herself to transforming our manuscript into a quality publication, assisted by the insights and careful editing of Rebecca Rauff. Cindy Flynn has been instrumental in designing advertising campaigns for both the 2006 *PreK–12 English Language Proficiency Standards* book and now this companion volume.

Above all, we cannot forget our immediate family members, who often sacrificed companionship so that our work could continue.

As our children have grown and developed over the past years, so has the thinking behind this book. We now are ready to share ideas for using the TESOL English language proficiency standards with the greater educational community. So, in closing, we dedicate this book to the many teachers and school leaders who have come to understand how standards-based education can make a difference for English language learners.

Margo Gottlieb, *Illinois Resource Center and WIDA Consortium*
Anne Katz, *School for International Training*
Gisela Ernst-Slavit, *Washington State University*

Introduction

The PreK–12 English Language Proficiency Standards

Standard 1: English language learners **communicate** for **social, intercultural,** and **instructional** purposes within the school setting

Standard 2: English language learners **communicate** information, ideas, and concepts necessary for academic success in the area of **language arts**

Standard 3: English language learners **communicate** information, ideas, and concepts necessary for academic success in the area of **mathematics**

Standard 4: English language learners **communicate** information, ideas, and concepts necessary for academic success in the area of **science**

Standard 5: English language learners **communicate** information, ideas, and concepts necessary for academic success in the area of **social studies**

Introduction

To have another language is to possess a second soul.
—Charlemagne

In 2006, in response to the changing political and educational context for English language learners in U.S. schools, TESOL published a revised set of language standards in *PreK–12 English Language Proficiency Standards*. These standards build on the theoretical framework set out in TESOL's 1997 English language standards (*ESL Standards for Pre-K–12 Students*) and exemplify the academic language that English language learners must develop in order to access the academic content of the general educational curriculum. The current volume, *Paper to Practice: Using the TESOL English Language Proficiency Standards in PreK–12 Classrooms*, serves as a companion to the 2006 standards by illustrating how educators in a variety of contexts can apply the standards to meet the diverse needs of their students.

Our purpose in *Paper to Practice* is to demonstrate how the English language proficiency (ELP) standards can function as a starting point for action in the classroom. The examples in each chapter suggest ways of using the ELP standards to improve instruction for English language learners within the framework of 21st-century classrooms. Today's teachers face daunting tasks that include understanding the complex nature of language as it is used in school, grappling with how to meet the diverse needs of their learners, creating lessons that help students access challenging academic content, and charting student progress in meeting the accountability criteria required of their schools.

Our premise is straightforward: Language is woven into the fabric of instruction. Understanding the multidimensionality of language and how it functions provides teachers with the means to support student achievement. When teachers have a thorough understanding of how language and content interact within school contexts, they are better equipped to make well-formed decisions about learning and teaching.

Content and organization

Paper to Practice consists of two sections. The first section presents an analysis of the language of school, provides an overview of the TESOL English language proficiency standards, and explores how the standards exemplify the academic language required for student achievement in school.

The second section builds on the resources found in section I by suggesting ways for educators to coordinate efforts in using the English language proficiency standards to develop instructional plans that are relevant to local school contexts. Specifically, it explores how the English language proficiency standards can be used when educators

- extend the usefulness of various elements of the standards matrices to meet individual classroom contexts

- collaborate to plan meaningful opportunities for English language learners to access content through language

- design curriculum and instruction that take into account students' English language proficiency levels

- create classroom-based assessment plans

Figure 1 illustrates the flow of these topics throughout the book.

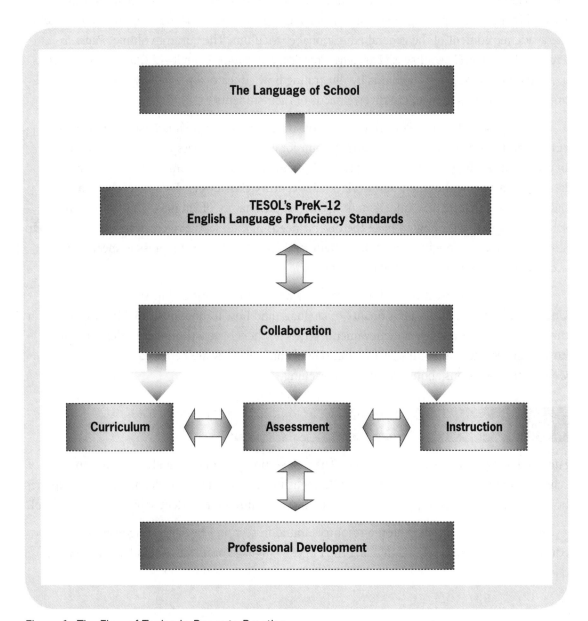

Figure 1. The Flow of Topics in *Paper to Practice.*

Approach

We explore the topics in Figure 1 as a means of assisting teachers, teacher educators, and others engaged in professional development. Our intent throughout *Paper to Practice* is to provide resources that will support personal reflection as well as teacher education in a variety of venues, including pre-service preparation programs and in-service workshops. The book includes the following features to assist in this endeavor:

- *Guiding Questions* provide structure for each chapter as well as a preview of the issues to be addressed. These questions may be used to stimulate discussion.

- *Vignettes* contextualize the content in classroom or school settings and illustrate the factors that affect teaching practice. We vary the classrooms portrayed because we recognize that English language learners are served via a variety of language education programs.

- *Tasks* sprinkled throughout each chapter make the content more useful for pre-service and in-service educators. The tasks are designed to engage readers in applications of the material—for example, by applying new ideas to their own teaching situations or by trying out standards-based techniques demonstrated in the chapter.

- *Reflect and Respond,* a section at the end of each chapter, is an opportunity to apply the key themes.

By incorporating these features, we emphasize the importance of professional development in disseminating the ELP standards and demonstrate ways of infusing the standards into curriculum, instruction, and assessment to make a cohesive and equitable educational system for all students.

Section I

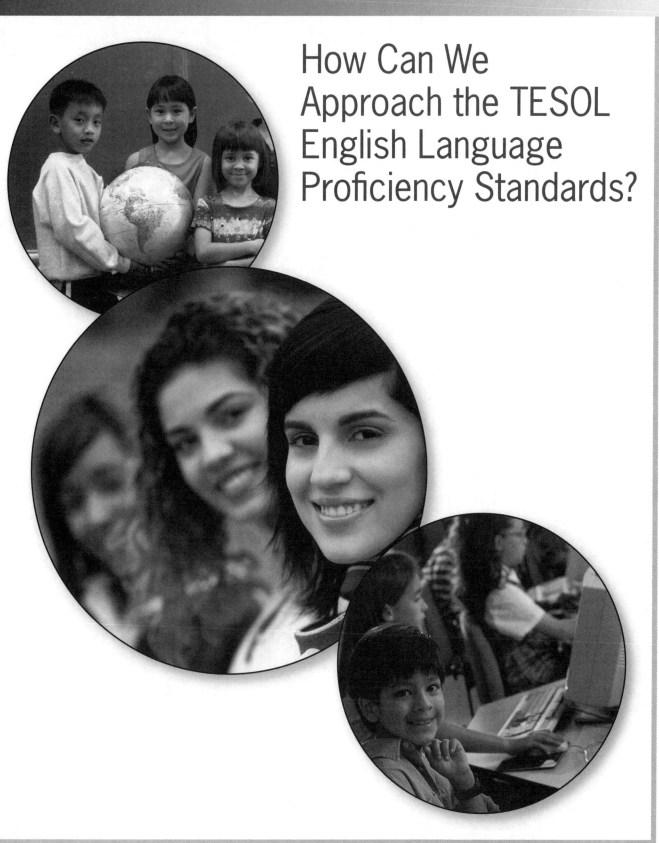

How Can We Approach the TESOL English Language Proficiency Standards?

Chapter 1
Rethinking the Language of School

Every teacher is a language teacher.

—Jeff Zwiers

Guiding Questions

➤ **What is the language of school?**

➤ **What is social language?**

➤ **What is academic language?**

➤ **What are the uses of social and academic language in school?**

➤ **What is the relationship between native languages and cultures?**

➤ **What is language proficiency in school?**

Everyday vocabulary words, such as *table, column, bat, glasses, sheet, letter,* and *pie,* can take on alternative meanings in the classroom. Although English language learners might know the meaning of *table* as a smooth, flat slab with legs, they might not know additional meanings used in content-specific contexts. For example, a *table* in the mathematics classroom can refer to a times table for multiplication facts or a table of values for graphing functions. *Table* may have additional meanings in other content areas, such as a timetable in social studies, a table of contents in language arts, a water table in physical science, and the periodic table in chemistry. If English language learners are to succeed in school, they need to become competent users of the specialized language associated with different academic disciplines. They must be able to understand the subtle nuances of language and apply multiple meanings of words and expressions to appropriate contexts and genres.

One way to facilitate the academic success of English language learners is to capitalize on the cultural as well as the academic knowledge and skills that students bring from their native lands and distinctive circumstances. By connecting new academic material with students' background knowledge and skills, educators can positively influence such affective factors as students' motivation, interest, and self-esteem, even in the unfamiliar setting of a U.S. school.

Uncovering the existing academic competencies of English language learners can provide a firm foundation upon which to build new content knowledge, skills, and thought processes. The native language competencies of English language learners represent a pre-existing academic skill as well as a resource that educators can utilize as a bridge to the students' second language development.

The language of school is the distinct, multifaceted type of English used primarily in classrooms. It is characterized by a broad range of language competencies necessary for students to fully participate in classroom activities and to function as members of content-centered communities. English language learners must develop competence in using social English to interact in the classroom while simultaneously acquiring the academic language associated with many specific content areas. Thus, both social and academic language proficiencies are part of the language of school and are necessary for school success.

Throughout *Paper to Practice*, we address the various influences on the development of English language proficiency, the specifics of content-area language, and the many factors affecting learners as they acquire the language of school. Figure 1.1 illustrates this interaction.

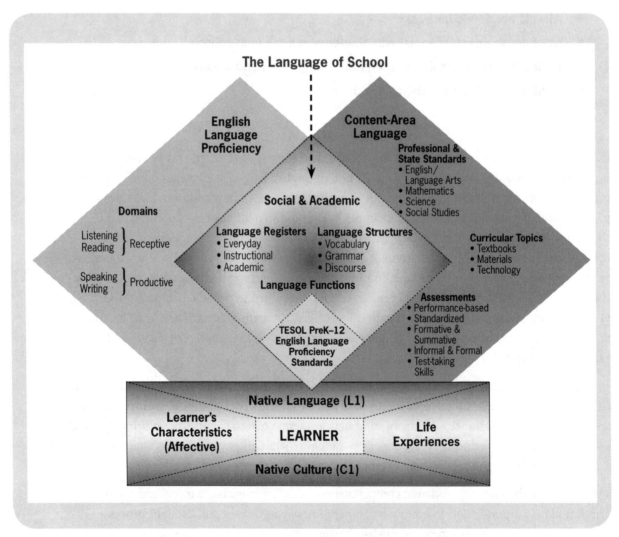

Figure 1.1. The Complexities of English Language Proficiency, Content-Area Language, and the Learner.

School is one of the places where, as suggested by Halliday (1993), people learn

- the *use* of language: how to speak, read, write, and listen to language
- *through* language: all about the world inside and outside the classroom
- *about* language: phonics, grammar, and spelling

For many students, particularly English language learners, schooling offers a new set of circumstances: a sometimes bewildering array of novel language experiences that include intercultural expectations and behaviors (*"Eyes on me!"*), ways of interacting (*"I am Mr. Arthur, your social studies teacher. Tell me one news event from this past week."*), and literacy demands (*"Compose a word problem for each equation, inequality, or expression."*). Figure 1.2 depicts three important aspects of the language of school: language registers, language structures, and language functions. These aspects are addressed in the following discussions of social and academic language.

Language registers

Language registers are the different varieties of language used depending on the setting, the relationship between the individuals involved in the communication, and the purpose of the interaction. For example, when students speak with teachers or adult relatives, they often use an entirely different style of communication than they do with their neighborhood friends. The language and gestures used with neighborhood friends are also different from those used when ordering at a local ice-cream parlor or speaking to the school principal. All students, including English language learners, need to develop a variety of language registers to successfully participate in *all* aspects of life.

In schools, as depicted in Figure 1.3, these registers can be organized into two broad categories—*social* and *academic*. Social language is the language needed for face-to-face interaction, chores and classroom routines, and communication with peers. This language, similar to the register used at home and on the playground, is necessary in the classroom and constitutes a foundation upon which other language registers can be built. Academic language,

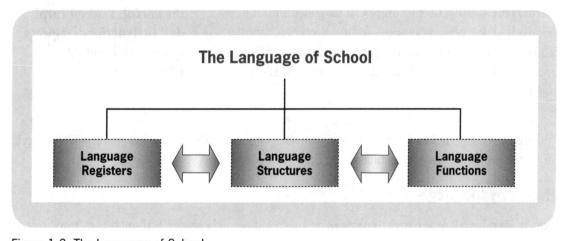

Figure 1.2. The Language of School.

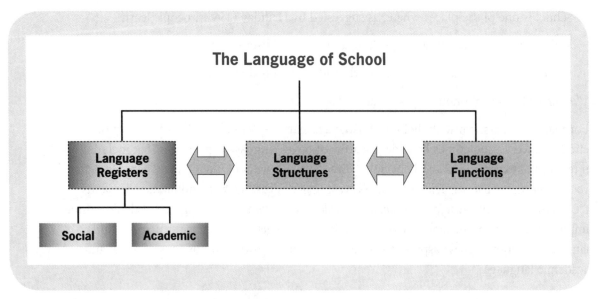

The Language of School

| Language Registers | ⟷ | Language Structures | ⟷ | Language Functions |

Language Registers:
- Social
- Academic

Figure 1.3. The Language Registers of School: Social and Academic.

on the other hand, is used to obtain, process, construct meaning from, and provide content-area information. It is primarily encountered in content-area classrooms and textbooks.

What are the differences between social language and academic language? Are they separate languages? Can they be learned at the same time? How quickly can they be learned? Although the distinctions between social and academic language are not precise, a description of each register is provided in the following sections.

➤ What is social language?

Social language includes the *everyday* and *instructional* registers used in face-to-face interactions within the school setting. Like all languages, it also includes intercultural aspects that are often subtle and nuanced. English language learners are capable of learning social language within a relatively quick period of time—around 2 years (Cummins, 2007). Although this is the language most often used during recess, in the hallway, and outside of school, it is also much needed in the classroom.

> *TESOL's English Language Proficiency Standard 1 focuses on the **social**, **intercultural**, and **instructional** aspects of English language competence.*

Teachers and students use social language for different purposes. As depicted in Figure 1.4, everyday language and instructional language are two ways in which social language is manifested in the classroom.

Everyday language

For English language learners to participate successfully in classroom activities, they must learn how to take turns in conversations with teachers and peers, how to ask for directions, and how to request materials. Examples of this kind of language are included in Figure 1.5.

Paper to Practice: Using the TESOL English Language Proficiency Standards in PreK–12 Classrooms

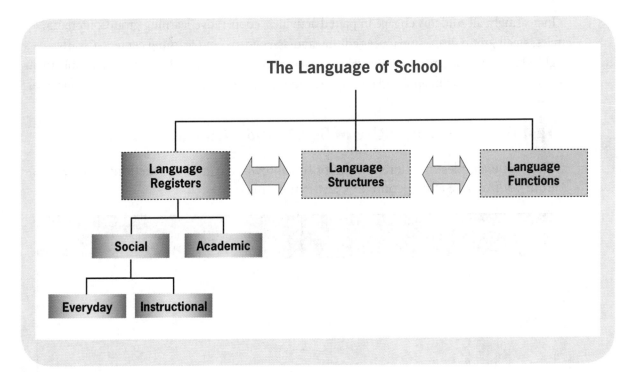

Figure 1.4. Social Language: Everyday and Instructional Uses.

Instructional language

Additionally, English language learners must acquire the nontechnical variety of English used in classrooms for instructional purposes or learning routines. Some examples include following directions, knowing when it is appropriate to raise one's hand or sharpen one's pencil, and understanding how and when to perform a task or complete an assignment. Figure 1.5 also includes examples of this kind of language.

Social Language	School-Related Examples
Everyday	"Can I play basketball with you?" "I'll trade you my apple for your cookie." "I'm almost late for class, and I can't get my locker open." "My brother and I watched a great movie over the weekend!"
Instructional	"Line up, single file." [routine command] "Please open your books to page 125." [instructional command] "Can anyone think of something people use today that might be similar to a _____ used during the time of _____?" [question] "The reason we do/wear _____ during a science experiment is because _____." [explanation]

Figure 1.5. Examples of the Social Language of School.

Increasingly, all students engage in paired activities, cooperative learning groups, literature circles, small group discussions, peer editing and assessment, and learning centers. Clearly, English language learners need to develop the social communication skills that will enable them to interact with others in appropriate ways across multiple settings and for a variety of purposes.

Task 1.1. A Teacher's Use of Social and Academic Language

Think of examples of different types of social (everyday and instructional) language from your own teaching context. List them in this chart:

Social Language	Examples
Everyday	
Instructional	

Task 1.2. What Students Need to Know and Say

Look at your examples of instructional language in Task 1.1 from a student's perspective. What language do students need to know to understand you and their other teachers? What do students need to say in response to your instructional language?

Social Language	Examples	
	Students Need to Know	**Students Need to Say**
Instructional		

➤ What is academic language?

Academic language is the language necessary for success in school. It is used to acquire new or deeper understandings of content related to the core curriculum areas, to communicate that understanding to others, and to participate effectively in the classroom environment. During instruction and assessment, students must be prepared to deal with a range of language demands—including both receptive and productive skills. *Receptive skills* involve the accessing of input:

> *TESOL's English Language Proficiency Standards 2, 3, 4, and 5 focus on the **academic** aspects of English language competence.*

- listening: understanding the teacher's oral language

- reading: accessing content from textbooks and other print materials

Productive skills involve creating ("do-ing") output:

- speaking: responding orally to academic tasks

- writing: creating written responses to content material

Academic language, also referred to as *academic English* or *content-specific language*, is a variety or register of English that is very different from social language. It is used in professional books and characterized by the specific linguistic features associated with academic disciplines (Scarcella, 2003b).

Particular aspects of academic language include

- specialized and technical vocabulary, including nuances and multiple meanings

- discourse associated with specific content areas or disciplines

- organization of genres

- linguistic complexity and density, and their related grammatical structures

- length and variety of utterances or written text

- multiple registers

- application of learning strategies and critical thinking skills

Yet, just as schools and learning contexts differ because of a host of factors, the features of academic language can vary by geographic region, content area, grade level, and individual teacher (Zwiers, 2008).

Language structures

Language spans several linguistic levels, including *language structures*, such as vocabulary, grammar, and discourse, and *language functions*—that is, the intent or purpose(s) of the communication. Each component highlighted in Figure 1.6 is discussed in this section.

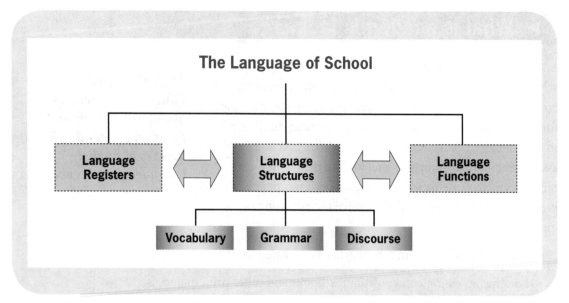

Figure 1.6. Language Structures: Vocabulary, Grammar, and Discourse.

Vocabulary

Vocabulary development is pivotal to content-area learning and provides a basis for learning from and creating meaningful written texts. Learning academic content is, in part, equivalent to understanding the key concepts and the words and phrases of each discipline. "Vocabulary is as unique to a content area as fingerprints are to a human being. A content area is distinguishable by its language, particularly the special and technical terms that label the concepts undergirding the subject matter" (Vacca & Vacca, 1999, p. 314).

Explicit vocabulary instruction—not in isolation, but within meaningful and relevant content-area instruction—has a positive effect on reading and content-area learning. Work by Allen (1999) and Nation (2001), among others, indicates that purposeful vocabulary instruction in the content areas (a) increases reading comprehension, (b) develops knowledge of new concepts, (c) improves range and specificity in writing, (d) helps students communicate more effectively, and (e) develops a deeper understanding of words and concepts. Figure 1.7 provides examples of the different types of vocabulary students need in order to participate in the content areas of language arts, mathematics, science, and social studies. The words are organized into three main categories: general vocabulary, specialized vocabulary, and technical vocabulary.

Grammar

At the sentence level, certain language patterns and grammatical structures occur frequently in individual content areas. These patterns are encountered primarily in textbooks and may be highly complex. Figure 1.8 provides examples of syntactic features that have distinctive uses in particular disciplines.

Discourse

Discourse refers to the ways in which oral and written language are organized. At the extended-text level, there are discipline-specific genres and general academic structures. Although genres

Types of Vocabulary	Language Arts	Mathematics	Science	Social Studies
General (not directly associated with a specific content area)	critical identity	digital restricted	summary demographic	
Specialized (associated with a content area)	adverb imagery proofreading	divisor equation graph	organism cell element	relief map abdicate diorama
Technical (associated with a specific content-area topic)	euphemism hyperbola logical fallacy	ratio integral Pythagorean theorem	photosynthesis enzyme eukaryotic cell	equatorial judicial branch floodplain

Figure 1.7. Examples of General, Specialized, and Technical Vocabulary by Content Area.

Language Arts	Mathematics	Science	Social Studies
hyperbole (*The river is so swift, the fish need motorboats to go upstream.*) onomatopoeia (*The honeybee buzzed as it flew from flower to flower.*) simile (*The waterfall shimmered across the face of the mountain like the glossy tail of a galloping horse.*)	logical connectors (*consequently, however*) comparative structures (*greater than, less than*) prepositions (*divided by, goes into*)	passive voice (*Three telescopes were built in Italy.*) grammatical metaphor (*The butterfly's changes are many.*) syntactic ambiguity (*Flying planes can be dangerous.*) complex noun phrases (*Life expectancy for laboratory-grown mice was higher than . . .*)	sequence words (*first, next, last, after*) historical present (*In his journal, Lewis writes that it is important to . . .*) causative signals (*as a result, thus, so*)

Figure 1.8. Examples of Syntactic Features by Content Area.

may vary according to the cultural context in which they are used, it is important to recognize that students are expected to produce certain text types in school (Schleppegrell, 2004). Figure 1.9 provides examples of discourse structures that are commonly found in specific content areas and suggests the challenges students face as they learn to recognize and analyze the discourse features of particular disciplines.

Language Arts	Mathematics	Science	Social Studies
narratives	tables	field notes	interviews
expository essays	proofs	lab reports	scenarios
critiques	graphs	research papers	historical descriptions
abstracts	problems	arguments	timelines
science fiction	explanations	explanations	travelogues

Figure 1.9. Examples of Discourse Used in Specific Content Areas.

Language functions

Language functions are an important component of the language of school (see Figure 1.10). They refer to how language is used in the communication of a message. Much of what is said in the classroom is for a purpose, such as greeting, congratulating, requesting permission to speak, requesting help, responding to a question, giving instructions, or explaining.

Figure 1.11 provides examples of language functions that are frequently used in specific content areas. If students are to be considered competent language users within the school setting, they must be able to use language functions according to the classroom demands.

➤ What are the uses of social and academic language in school?

Although English language learners may acquire *social* language proficiency in just 1 or 2 years, it takes 4–7 years of sustained institutional support for students to access and gain command of the *academic* registers needed for success in school (Cummins, 2005; Tsang, Katz, & Stack, 2008).

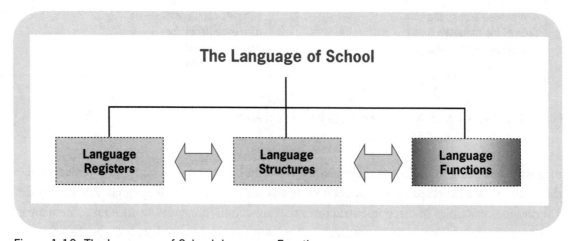

Figure 1.10. The Language of School: Language Functions.

Language Arts	Mathematics	Science	Social Studies
predicting	explaining	hypothesizing	seeking information
debating	justifying	defining	sequencing
composing reviews	following directions	comparing	contrasting
narrating stories	listing traits	describing phenomena	role-playing

Figure 1.11. Examples of Language Functions Used in Specific Content Areas.

In clarifying the distinctive characteristics and attributes of academic language, Scarcella and Rumberger (2000) identify five main differences between social and academic language. We've summarized these aspects of language proficiency in our Figure 1.12. Although social and academic language may not always appear as a dichotomy but rather as two ends of a continuum, the contrast between these two types of language illustrates some essential features of the language used in school settings.

Aspect of Proficiency	Social Language	Academic Language
Language Domains	often relies on listening and speaking	primarily relies on reading and writing
Accuracy	accepts minor errors	requires a high degree of accuracy in grammar and vocabulary
Language Functions	primarily relies on narrative functions such as describing, telling, and relating	relies on more complex functions such as persuading, arguing, interpreting, and hypothesizing
Cognitive Demands	is often less demanding and highly contextualized	is cognitively demanding and often decontextualized, requiring prior knowledge of vocabulary, grammar, and conventions
Vocabulary and Grammar	involves a smaller range of vocabulary and structures	requires knowledge of thousands of words and how to use them

Figure 1.12. Perceived Differences Between Social and Academic Language.

Task 1.3. Use of Academic Language in School

Consider ways you can focus on academic language in your teaching context. Use the table below to answer these questions:

- List some everyday vocabulary words such as *meter*, *tree*, and *column* that have additional specific meanings in a content area. What activities or events would allow students to practice and use these terms within an academic context?

- What language functions are specific to your teaching context? Which ones are shared with other content areas?

- Think about specific grammatical structures that students need to know in your classroom. How or when do your students learn these structures? How could you explicitly teach them? Are these structures specific to certain content areas?

- What kinds of discourse do students learn in your teaching context? How do you teach them? Are these discourse structures the same as or different from other types that students must learn?

	Examples of Academic Language Use
Vocabulary	
Language Functions	
Grammatical Structures	
Discourse	

➤ What is the relationship between native languages and cultures?

Intercultural aspects of language in the classroom

Language simultaneously mirrors culture and is influenced and formed by it. In a broad sense, language is a symbolic representation of a cultural group, reflecting its history and its ways of doing things. The languages of school—both social and academic—refer to more than just the ability of students to produce appropriate language registers, language structures, and language functions. Less visible linguistic components such as cultural knowledge about ways to interact in diverse school situations are equally important.

For example, participation in structured activities such as storytelling and "show-and-tell" requires linguistic knowledge but also cultural knowledge about *how* to participate. A simple activity such as storytelling can vary from culture to culture. In some cultures, audience participation is expected and necessary, while in others the expectation is to have a captive yet silent audience. Within the Arapaho community, for example, a good story is one that continues day after day. This way of telling a story contrasts sharply with the linear line of thought—featuring a distinct beginning, middle, and end—omnipresent in preK–12 classrooms.

Tapping students' native languages and cultures

English language learners are already familiar with their native languages and have an intuitive understanding of the structural and functional characteristics of language. This knowledge can contribute greatly to their successful development of English language skills. In fact, research indicates that full proficiency in the native language facilitates the development of a second language (August & Hakuta, 1998; Baker, 2001) and can play a significant role in learning complex material such as that typically encountered in content-area classrooms (Ernst-Slavit & Slavit, 2007; Hornberger, 2003). The key is to consider students' native languages and cultures as resources to be tapped and integrated into the teaching and learning process.

Task 1.4. Intercultural Aspects of Classroom Talk

Think about embedded U.S. cultural knowledge that immigrant students must learn to recognize and produce for success in the classroom. Fill in the chart with examples from your own teaching experience that illustrate how intercultural aspects of classroom talk can hinder or enhance communication and learning.

Instructional Expectations	Background Influences
Example: "Eyes on me."	*Example: In some cultures, children show respect by looking down when addressed by an adult.*

Language proficiency in school is multidimensional; in addition to linguistic and sociocultural factors, it entails cognitive factors. All these factors, as illustrated in Figure 1.13 and discussed in *PreK–12 English Language Proficiency Standards* (TESOL, 2006), operate both inside and outside the classroom and influence the acquisition of a second, third, or fourth language. In other words, English language proficiency represents English language learners' entire range of experiences with and interactions using their new language.

More specifically, *linguistic* factors are critical in the development of language proficiency. They refer to the array of language features required of English language learners for successful communication in school. These features include phonology, grammar, and semantics as well as sociolinguistic and discourse components. *Sociocultural* factors include contextual influences that have an impact on students' ability to use language in school. The role of affect, such as attitudes, motivation, investment, and resilience, as well as the influence of students' native languages and cultures, has a direct impact on language development and proficiency.

Language proficiency in school also involves a *cognitive* dimension. To be successful in school, English language learners need to use a variety of learning strategies that facilitate higher order thinking and draw on their metalinguistic and metacognitive awareness. Throughout this book, vignettes and examples illustrate the roles played by cognitive, linguistic, and sociocultural factors in the development of language proficiency and, ultimately, in school achievement.

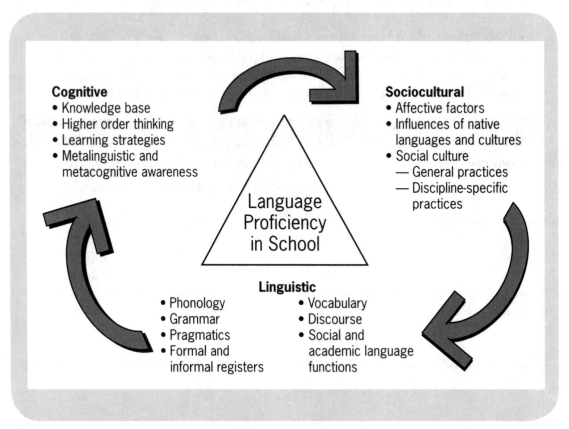

Figure 1.13. Language Proficiency in School: Cognitive, Sociocultural, and Linguistic Dimensions. Reprinted from *PreK–12 English Language Proficiency Standards* (TESOL, 2006, p. 17).

To be successful in school, English language learners must learn a new culture and a new language, including a variety of registers. The language of school is characterized by a broad range of language competencies necessary for English language learners to participate fully in classroom and school activities. Although students first learn *social* English to interact with others on the playground, in the neighborhood, and in the classroom, they must also acquire the *academic* language associated with each content area.

Often educators use simplified texts (both oral and written) with their English language learners as a way of making the content accessible for students. This practice, however, might deprive students of opportunities to be exposed to and learn the specific, connected discourse style that characterizes the language of a particular content area. In addition, simplified texts might not provide students with all the information required to understand the material and to successfully demonstrate mastery of the topic. In order to succeed in school, English language learners need to be exposed to and learn both the social and the academic language required in various content areas through the use of grade-level-appropriate materials and resources.

Reflect and Respond

The language of school may be totally unfamiliar to English language learners. It is as complex as it is distinctive, representing the interaction among language registers, language structures, and language functions.

Now that you have read about the complexity of school language, consider the kinds of language your students need in order to access their academic content.

List all the ways you promote academic language development in your classroom.

How do you ensure that English language learners have a variety of opportunities to hear, read, and use academic language? Give some examples from your classroom or experience.

Chapter 2
Using the English Language Proficiency Standards to Integrate Language and Content

If we spoke a different language, we would perceive a somewhat different world.

—Ludwig Wittgenstein

Guiding Questions

➤ **What is the relationship between academic language and content?**

➤ **What are the principles of academic language proficiency that underlie the TESOL English language proficiency standards?**

➤ **What is the relationship between the TESOL English language proficiency standards and academic content standards?**

Vignette

It was late. The kids were in bed, and second-grade teacher Emily Major was working on an upcoming science unit. In her 12 years of teaching experience, she had memories of students she would never forget, but nothing had prepared her for this year.

Never had she worked so hard, felt so rewarded, yet realized that so much need remained. Perhaps these feelings stemmed from the fact that 7 of her 28 students were receiving language support services and another 6 had recently exited from the English language learner (ELL) program. Perhaps it was the sense of awe she experienced every time she heard five different languages being spoken in her room during activities. Or perhaps her feelings stemmed from the frustrations and joys of helping Marisol, her new Kanjobal Mayan student from rural Guatemala.

Although she was confident of her overall teaching skills, Emily still struggled to successfully apply what she knew about ESL in an intentional manner designed to develop content-area skills as well as English language proficiency. How could the TESOL preK–12 English language proficiency standards be of assistance as Emily planned instruction for her students?

➤ What is the relationship between academic language and content?

The development of specific content-area academic language is a critical component of developing understanding within a content area. For example, students in a biology class studying genetics need to know the vocabulary, grammar, distinctive language functions, genres, and discourse styles specific to this topic. If students are to participate in a lab experiment and be able to answer questions on the topic of genetics, they must be able to

- use and understand academic vocabulary such as *fungus, prediction, spore, crossbreed, genotype, phenotype,* and *petri dish*

- access a variety of texts on genetics

- write and answer questions

- conduct interviews

- organize and keep track of their data

- describe phenomena

- compare their results to hypotheses

- collaborate in heterogeneous groups

- summarize their findings

- complete lab reports or maintain learning logs

- plan and make presentations to the whole class

Clearly, students in a content-area class such as biology must be ready to manipulate a wide range of specific linguistic features associated with the particular content area.

➤ What are the principles of academic language proficiency that underlie the TESOL English language proficiency standards?

Current research and practice have influenced the development of the TESOL English language proficiency (ELP) standards. The principles that serve as the foundation for the ELP standards represent our vision of the role of language proficiency—specifically, academic language proficiency—in the language and literacy development of English language learners. These principles are stated in Figure 2.1.

In this section we explain Principles 1–5, as found in *PreK–12 English Language Proficiency Standards* (TESOL, 2006, p. 19), and we introduce a sixth principle.

Principle	Description
1	Language proficiency is an outgrowth of cumulative experiences both inside and outside of school.
2	Language proficiency can reflect complex thinking when linguistic complexity is reduced and support is present.
3	Both social and academic language proficiencies are necessary for school success.
4	Academic language proficiency works in tandem with academic achievement.
5	Academic language proficiency is developed through sustained content-based language instruction.
6	Native language proficiency—in particular, academic language proficiency in the native language—facilitates the acquisition of academic language proficiency in English.

Figure 2.1. Principles of Language Proficiency. Adapted from *PreK–12 English Language Proficiency Standards* (TESOL, 2006, p. 19).

Principle 1: Language proficiency is an outgrowth of cumulative experiences both inside and outside of school.

Many English language learners experience and interact in English throughout the day. Outside of school, students may use everyday English with their siblings or friends, serve as translators for family members, have jobs where English is required, or simply watch TV. These opportunities facilitate English language learners' acquisition of social language proficiency. In school, teachers can build upon the students' background and knowledge, including the linguistically and culturally based perspectives they bring to the classroom, while introducing new experiences to extend students' academic language proficiency.

> *By spring, Emily's student Ernesto was still struggling with reading. To motivate him, Emily located and read with him a book about a Latino boy who celebrated his birthday by eating cake and hitting a piñata with family and friends. Although Ernesto expressed interest in the story, reading continued to be difficult for him. While discussing the story, Ernesto excitedly told Emily all about his most recent birthday party, during which he had celebrated just like the boy in the book. Thinking that this connection might be used to support Ernesto's literacy skills, Emily asked Ernesto if he would like to make a book about his experience, similar to the one they had just finished reading. Ernesto's eyes lit up, and he eagerly agreed.*

With the assistance of a parent volunteer, Ernesto completed his book that same day. Over the next few days, Ernesto proudly read to others from his book—a book based on his own personal experiences.

Principle 2: Language proficiency can reflect complex thinking when linguistic complexity is reduced and support is present.

There is a relationship between language and cognition; however, students' skill level in a language does not need to limit their level of thinking. In other words, students at the early stages of English language acquisition can demonstrate complex thinking even if they must use simple language. Teachers can implement this principle by using strategies and instructional supports that enable their students to engage meaningfully in the learning process, even at the earliest stages of English language proficiency.

For example, consider the language a beginning-level second-grade student might need to know and draw on in reading about science. A strand of sample performance indicators reprinted in Figure 2.2 from *PreK–12 English Language Proficiency Standards* (TESOL, 2006) shows that students at Language Proficiency Levels 1 and 2 are engaged in the academic tasks of sorting and sequencing information related to a grade-level academic content topic. The language required for these tasks can be adjusted to the English language proficiency levels of the students while retaining higher levels of academic engagement.

Domain	Topic	Level 1	Level 2	Level 3	Level 4	Level 5
READING	Life cycles Water cycle Organisms and environments	Match pictures with labels (e.g., tadpoles/frogs, caterpillars/butterflies)	Sequence phases of cycles or associate pictures with phases using graphic support	Draw or select responses to visually or graphically supported descriptive paragraphs about phases or stages in cycles	Categorize extended text according to illustrated phases or stages of processes (e.g., in the food chain)	Compare information about various cycles or organisms and apply analysis to new contexts

Figure 2.2. A Strand of Sample Performance Indicators From Standard 4, the Language of Science. Reprinted from *PreK–12 English Language Proficiency Standards* (TESOL, 2006, p. 65).

Principle 3: Both social and academic language proficiencies are necessary for school success.

Language proficiency represents the full repertoire of language use. Social and academic language proficiencies often develop simultaneously in the context of school. Teachers must be aware of the social language demands of school (the casual and instructional situations students face) in addition to the language students need to access content and succeed academically.

After reviewing the TESOL ELP standards as well as her state's English language development standards, Emily thought over her upcoming science unit on the characteristics of animals. She quickly divided a sheet of paper into three columns, labeling them general vocabulary, specialized vocabulary, and technical vocabulary. Then she quieted her mind, tried to put herself in her English language learners' shoes, and started writing.

Under general vocabulary, she included words and phrases her students would need in order to collaborate successfully in heterogeneous groups regardless of the content area. The specialized vocabulary column contained words pertinent to the overall science topic under investigation. In the technical vocabulary column, Emily listed highly specific words integral to her unit on animal characteristics. Emily had already prioritized the vocabulary, concepts, and skills from her required curriculum when she originally planned this science unit.

After a few minutes, her paper appeared as follows:

General Vocabulary	Specialized Vocabulary	Technical Vocabulary
polite phrases (please, thank you, excuse me)	animal names (frog, horse, lizard, salamander, snake, turtle)	mammal, reptile, amphibian
tools (grid, chart, graph)	characteristic	nocturnal, diurnal
team	continent	migration, hibernation
jobs or roles (artist, director, expert, specialist)	habitat, inhabit	desert, rain forest, veld, wetland
sort, group, classify	reproduce, reproduction	oviparous, ovoviviparous
describe, description	food source	herbivore, omnivore, predator, scavenger
look like, appear, observe, see	evidence, data, facts, feathers, fur, scales	exoskeleton, endoskeleton

That was the easy part: Nouns, verbs, useful phrases . . . basic vocabulary was relatively easy to identify.

Next, Emily thought about specific English language development goals and how her students would need to use the language functionally. She took out another piece of paper and wrote the following:

Language Function	Application
cite information	This _____ explains/shows that _____.
compare	This _____ is similar to that _____ because _____.
contrast	This _____ is different from that _____ because one _____ and the other doesn't _____.
demonstrate cause and effect	The _____ had _____, so _____.
describe	The _____ has _____ and _____.
draw conclusions	On the basis of _____, I conclude that _____.
hypothesize	If _____ had _____, then _____ would have _____.
retell	First, _____. Next, _____, and then _____.

A sudden idea about how to set up cooperative groups based on literature circles came to mind, and Emily began another chart:

Student Role	Description
project director	
media specialist	
graphic artist	
LOTE (language other than English) expert/writer	

Emily still needed to define what she expected from each group member in the science class, but her notes provided a good start—and her plans would encourage students to practice the speaking, listening, reading, and writing skills necessary for academic language development. Although Emily had more work to do on the entire unit in order to make it accessible for her English language learners, she was on track and satisfied with her progress. Tomorrow she would work on the unit again.

Principle 4: Academic language proficiency works in tandem with academic achievement.

Academic language proficiency is a vital component of academic achievement. Students need academic language in order to understand and express themselves in content-area classes. Attaching the academic language to the skills and knowledge required in the content area makes academic achievement more readily accessible for English language learners.

Mastery of academic language is needed by all students for long-term success in the core content areas (Francis, Lesaux, Kieffer, & Rivera, 2006; Scarcella, 2003a). Although factors such as motivation, learning strategies, persistence, literacy skills and habits, and study skills play an important part in the learning process, language plays the pivotal role in determining students' academic success. Academic language proficiency provides a pathway to academic achievement.

Language proficiency refers to the level of competence at which an individual is able to use language both for basic communicative tasks and for academic purposes. In contrast, *academic achievement* focuses on the knowledge and skills students must demonstrate in each core content area. As Figure 2.3 illustrates, *academic language proficiency* is represented as the interaction between language proficiency and academic achievement.

Principle 5: Academic language proficiency is developed through sustained content-based language instruction.

For many English language learners, academic language proficiency in English develops mostly in the school setting. To reach the full proficiency necessary for academic success, English language learners must receive initial and continuing school-based language support. The TESOL English language proficiency standards offer ways for educators to assist students in accessing content through language in the core content areas. Thus, through content-based language instruction, all teachers share the responsibility for educating English language learners.

As discussed in chapter 1, academic language proficiency encompasses all aspects of language that intersect with content, such as vocabulary, grammatical structures, genres and discourse styles, and use of multiple registers.

Academic language proficiency drives content-based curriculum and instruction for English language learners. For students to achieve success in the content areas, they will have to "talk" the language of each content area (Lemke, 1990). That is, they will need to use specific academic language to learn and express content-area knowledge (Slavit & Ernst-Slavit, 2007).

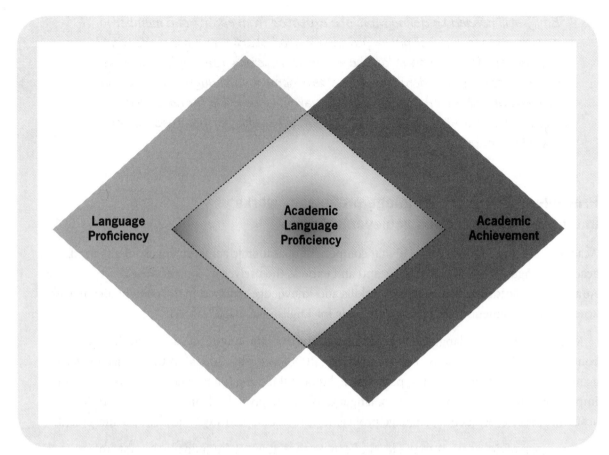

Figure 2.3. Academic Language Proficiency: The Intersection of Language Proficiency and Academic Achievement. Adapted from Gottlieb (2003, p. 12).

In educational contexts, the connection between academic language proficiency and academic achievement is of great importance. As depicted in Figure 2.4, academic language proficiency and academic achievement share similar features; however, they have distinct differences.

Principle 6: Native language proficiency—in particular, academic language proficiency in the native language—facilitates the acquisition of academic language proficiency in English.

English language learners whose first or native language is strongly developed—especially those with good literacy skills—have foundational knowledge and skills that readily transfer to a new language (Genesee, Lindholm-Leary, Saunders, & Christian, 2006). In addition, depending on the native language, cognates may give students useful insights into meaning. Cognates are words in one language that are similar in meaning and form to words in another language. For example, Spanish-speaking students often understand more English than they realize because there are about 4,000 cognates in English and Spanish. As Figure 2.5 illustrates, many of these cognates are much-needed terms in content-area studies.

Academic Language Proficiency	Academic Achievement
is language-based	is content-based
reflects the varying stages of second language acquisition	reflects conceptual development
represents both social and academic language	represents the school's academic curriculum
is tied to a state's English language proficiency standards	is tied to a state's academic content standards

Figure 2.4. Comparison of Academic Language Proficiency and Academic Achievement.

With a solid conceptual base in their native language, students can more readily recognize, comprehend, and apply new vocabulary and language patterns in a second language. As a result, English language learners with native language proficiency often acquire English at a faster pace and reach higher levels of English language proficiency. These higher levels of proficiency can be reached in all content areas and in diverse educational settings with intentional instruction and consistent, effective support for English language learners.

English	Spanish
circle	círculo
sarcastic	sarcástico
lateral	lateral
quadrilateral	cuadrilátero
edifice	edificio
genetics	genética
testament	testamento
aristocracy	aristocracia
marine biology	biología marina
adverb	adverbio
economy	economía

Figure 2.5. Examples of Academic Cognates in English and Spanish.

Task 2.1. Needs Assessment of Learning Contexts for English Language Learners

Consider the environment for English language learners in your teaching context, and conduct your own needs assessment. Look over the list of principles and think about the instructional practices and resources that are available to your students. Put a checkmark next to the principles you feel are being implemented and provide examples of how they are being implemented. Put an exclamation mark next to the principles that need work.

Principles of Language Proficiency	Already Implemented (✔)	Examples of How Principles Are Being Implemented	Needs Work (!)
Principle 1. Language proficiency is an outgrowth of cumulative experiences both inside and outside of school.			
Principle 2. Language proficiency can reflect complex thinking when linguistic complexity is reduced and support is present.			
Principle 3. Both social and academic language proficiencies are necessary for school success.			
Principle 4. Academic language proficiency works in tandem with academic achievement.			
Principle 5. Academic language proficiency is developed through sustained content-based language instruction.			
Principle 6. Native language proficiency—in particular, academic language proficiency in the native language—facilitates the acquisition of academic language proficiency in English.			

The TESOL English language proficiency standards are grounded in national and state ESL and academic content standards. (See pages 123–125 of *PreK–12 English Language Proficiency Standards* [TESOL, 2006] for a list of the source documents used in developing the TESOL ELP standards.) Figure 2.6 lists the national organizations whose academic content standards were consulted. Because national standards define the range of competencies within each content area, those standards were used to select the topics in the development of the sample performance indicators for the TESOL English language proficiency standards.

The sample performance indicators provided in *PreK–12 English Language Proficiency Standards* (TESOL, 2006, pp. 45–97) are based on and aligned with state and national academic content standards. The alignment process entailed a comprehensive survey and content analysis of national and state standards in the core content areas of language arts, mathematics, science, and social studies. As Figure 2.7 illustrates, this survey and analysis yielded common topics. Lists of these topics at the benchmark grades for each grade-level cluster (K, 3, 5, 8, and 12) were generated and used in developing the strands of sample performance indicators. These lists of academic content topics are reprinted in Appendix A.

Focus of TESOL's English Language Proficiency Standards	Source of Academic Content Standards
1. Communication in English for social, intercultural, and instructional purposes	Teachers of English to Speakers of Other Languages, Inc.
2. Communication of information, ideas, and concepts of language arts	National Council of Teachers of English and International Reading Association
3. Communication of information, ideas, and concepts of mathematics	National Council of Teachers of Mathematics
4. Communication of information, ideas, and concepts of science	National Research Council
5. Communication of information, ideas, and concepts of social studies	National Council for the Social Studies

Figure 2.6. Anchors for the TESOL English Language Proficiency Standards. Reprinted from *PreK–12 English Language Proficiency Standards* (TESOL, 2006, p. 25).

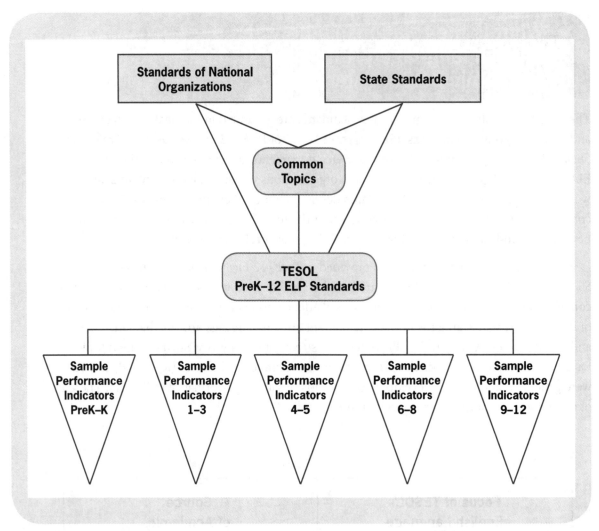

Figure 2.7. Process Used to Formulate Sample Performance Indicators for the TESOL English Language Proficiency Standards.

Task 2.2. Comparison of Standards

Locate the state academic content standards that are relevant to your teaching context. Then look at the academic content topics in Appendix A. Find the topics that appear in both sets of standards.

Paper to Practice: Using the TESOL English Language Proficiency Standards in PreK–12 Classrooms

Reflect and Respond

This chapter discusses the relationships among language, content, and language proficiency within the context of academic achievement. It also explains how the TESOL ELP standards connect with national and state academic content standards.

Select one topic from the academic content standards for your state or district or from the list of content topics in Appendix A. Plan a lesson or activity for the topic, keeping a list of all the language features that students need to use if they are to participate successfully in this lesson or activity. Include vocabulary, language functions, grammatical structures, and discourse styles.

Vignette Revisited

After completing her science unit, Emily Major was busy collecting her materials as the students left her classroom.

"Good-bye, Mrs. Major. I really enjoyed science this week. See you Monday!" shouted Joel on his way out the door to the bus.

Quietly, Marisol waited for Emily's attention. Eyes sparkling with delight, she stated, "Me gusta science!" With a wave and a shy but happy smile, Marisol ran to meet her mother.

"Ich auch, Mrs. Major," asserted Günther.

Tired but immensely pleased, Emily Major reflected on what had worked well, what needed improvement, and what new English language development ideas she should incorporate in her forthcoming social studies unit. With everyone in the classroom working together as a community of learners, supporting and valuing the linguistic and cultural resources of all students, her classroom had become a safe place to experiment with language, difficult concepts, and cultural norms.

Smiling to herself, Emily pulled out her social studies unit and set to work.

Chapter 3
Focusing on the Framework and Components of the English Language Proficiency Standards

The difference between the right word and the almost right word is the difference between lightning and a lightning bug.

—Mark Twain

Guiding Questions

➤ What information about English language learners helps guide educators in implementing standards-based education?

➤ How do the performance definitions frame the TESOL English language proficiency standards?

➤ How are the components of the TESOL English language proficiency standards organized?

➤ What are the elements of the sample performance indicators, and how are they presented in the strands?

Vignette

Lila Gómez, an English language learner (ELL) coach in a rural elementary district, was familiar with her state's English language proficiency and academic content standards. She had recently participated in a regional professional development workshop where the TESOL English language proficiency standards were introduced as an added resource to the state standards. Lila was the sole ELL coach in her district, so it was her responsibility to disseminate information about the TESOL standards to general education teachers working with the heterogeneous mix of English language learners sprinkled across the schools.

Lila asked herself, "Where do I begin to explain the complexity of these standards to teachers who aren't familiar with them?" She decided to start by providing an overview of the second language acquisition process and showing how it was captured in the performance definitions of the five levels of English language proficiency. From there, Lila planned to share the English language proficiency standards and identify the components of their framework. Through continued discussion with the teachers at grade-level meetings, she hoped to encourage groups across the district to begin integrating the TESOL English language proficiency standards into their current practices.

The TESOL English language proficiency (ELP) standards help define the language appropriate for English language learners within a grade-level cluster at each stage of language proficiency. Although the standards highlight students' development of academic language proficiency, they acknowledge the importance of social language proficiency along with its intercultural implications and applications.

Paper to Practice stresses the language side of standards-based teaching for English language learners. The TESOL ELP standards emphasize language within social and academic contexts as follows:

- Standard 1 focuses on social, intercultural, and instructional *language*.

- Standard 2 focuses on the *language* of language arts.

- Standard 3 focuses on the *language* of mathematics.

- Standard 4 focuses on the *language* of science.

- Standard 5 focuses on the *language* of social studies.

In this chapter, we review the format of the TESOL ELP standards; much of the information is recast from *PreK–12 English Language Proficiency Standards* (TESOL, 2006) to reacquaint readers with the basic components of the standards matrix. We explain the role of the performance definitions as a companion to the standards in order to show how the two structures complement each other. Chapter 4 provides a more in-depth analysis of the matrix components with suggestions for use.

Before reviewing the standards matrix, we examine the characteristics of second language learners that may influence how teachers implement the ELP standards.

➤ What information about English language learners helps guide educators in implementing standards-based education?

English language learners are a tremendously heterogeneous group of students, bringing to school diverse linguistic and cultural backgrounds and experiences. Their distinctive characteristics must be taken into account when thinking about how to craft standards-based curriculum, instruction, and assessment. Understanding their students' diversity can help teachers set realistic goals for the students' language learning.

Effective use of the ELP standards includes taking individual student characteristics into account. For example, the grade-level discourse of 6-year-olds, irrespective of their language proficiency, does not resemble that of 15-year-olds; these age and maturation differences affect instructional practices. Likewise, the experiences of Hmong children, as an example, vary greatly from those of Somali children—which in turn are vastly different from those of most other English language learners. Gifted and talented English language learners and those diagnosed with learning disabilities are other subgroups whose distinct needs must be considered when using the TESOL ELP standards. Some student characteristics that may affect language learning include

- maturation and personality traits (e.g., motivation, shyness)

- language and cultural heritage

- family mobility

- refugee or immigrant status

- socioeconomic status

- learning differences

Student data provide additional information to shape the design of standards-based instruction and assessment. Students with strong educational backgrounds in their native language differ substantially from those coming into the classroom with limited or interrupted formal schooling. Data regarding the students' proficiency in their native language and in English, along with information on their academic achievement, offer insight into the extent of their language development and learning. Together, student characteristics and student data constitute the backdrop to a standards-based language program. Relevant student data include

- prior educational experiences (e.g., continuity of language education, languages of instruction, locations)

- available school attendance data

- native language (L1) proficiency, including oral and literacy development

- native language achievement

- English (L2) language proficiency

- progress in L2 (and L1) proficiency over time

Task 3.1. Student Characteristics and Data

Think about the English language learners in your setting. What characteristics do they have that may affect the way you construct teaching and learning experiences? What student data are available to help you craft standards-based instruction and assessment? Use a chart like this one to identify relevant factors for your students.

Factors That Affect Teaching and Learning for English Language Learners	
Student Characteristics	
Student Data	

Lila's district had English language learners in kindergarten through Grade 5 from over a dozen countries and 15 language groups. At one school she had even discovered a set of twins who had recently been adopted from a Russian orphanage. To improve communication between schools, Lila worked diligently with the computer programmers to insert relevant information about English language learners into the district's database. In that way, teachers and administrators could share student characteristics and relevant student data.

➤ How do the performance definitions frame the TESOL English language proficiency standards?

Gathering information about English language learners is the first step in instructional planning. Understanding of the students' demographic and historical backgrounds provides the context in which language education program goals and standards are operationalized (Gottlieb & Nguyen, 2007). Next, we examine the criteria associated with the performance definitions to ascertain the expectations for each level of English language proficiency.

The performance definitions outline how English language learners process and use language across the language domains and standards for each level of language proficiency. As a complement to the standards matrix, the performance definitions describe language features to convey an overall estimate of where students are on their pathway to becoming proficient in English.

The features of the performance definitions are drawn from the language of school, as described in chapter 1. The definitions consist of four interrelated criteria that scaffold, or build upon each other, with each successive level of language proficiency. The criteria include

- *social and academic language functions:* the purposes of the communication or message; in other words, descriptions of how students use language

- *vocabulary:* general, specialized, or technical words, phrases, and expressions associated with content

- *grammatical structures:* the language patterns specific to individual content areas

- *discourse:* general academic structures and discipline-specific genres; a term used to describe relatively large chunks of conversation or connected written text

The performance definitions apply equally to social, intercultural, and academic settings. Together the performance definitions and the ELP standards capture the full repertoire of the language demands of school. Figure 3.1 illustrates the performance definitions for the five English language proficiency levels, with callouts highlighting the four criteria.

Level 1 Starting	Level 2 Emerging	Level 3 Developing	Level 4 Expanding	Level 5 Bridging	
English language learners can understand and use ...					
... language to communicate with others around basic concrete needs.	... language to draw on simple and routine experiences to communicate with others.	... language to communicate with others on familiar matters regularly encountered.	... language in both concrete and abstract situations and apply language to new experiences.	... a wide range of longer oral and written texts and recognize implicit meaning.	**Language Functions**
... high-frequency words and memorized chunks of language.	... high-frequency and some general academic vocabulary and expressions.	... general and some specialized academic vocabulary and expressions.	... specialized and some technical academic vocabulary and expressions.	... technical academic vocabulary and expressions.	**Vocabulary**
... words, phrases, or chunks of language.	... phrases or short sentences in oral or written communication.	... expanded sentences in oral or written communication.	... a variety of sentence lengths of varying linguistic complexity in oral and written communication.	... a variety of sentence lengths of varying linguistic complexity in extended oral or written discourse.	**Grammatical Structures**
... pictorial, graphic, or nonverbal representation of language.	... oral or written language, making errors that often impede the meaning of the communication.	... oral or written language, making errors that may impede the communication but retain much of its meaning.	... oral or written language, making minimal errors that do not impede the overall meaning of the communication.	... oral or written language approaching comparability to that of English-proficient peers.	**Discourse**

Figure 3.1. Performance Definitions of the Five Levels of English Language Proficiency. Adapted from *PreK–12 English Language Proficiency Standards* (TESOL, 2006, p. 39).

Task 3.2. Performance Definitions for the TESOL ELP Standards

The performance definitions provide overarching criteria that are descriptive of the five ELP levels. As such, they are general indicators of student performance. Think about how you might use these definitions to help you analyze your instructional practices.

Consider, for example, the language required by

- the tasks you assign your students

- the textbooks and other materials they use

- the tests and other methods of assessment used to measure their learning

- teacher talk

How well do these language demands match the language proficiency levels of the students in your class as described in the performance definitions?

Lila was perplexed. Her state's English language development standards and performance definitions didn't match TESOL's ELP standards and performance definitions. She realized that the TESOL standards, which exemplified the language of the core content areas across language domains, were more comprehensive in their description of the language of content-area discourse. To reconcile the dilemma, Lila thought about having teachers use a Venn diagram (see Figure 3.2) to gain a deeper understanding of the structure of the standards-based system for their English language learners.

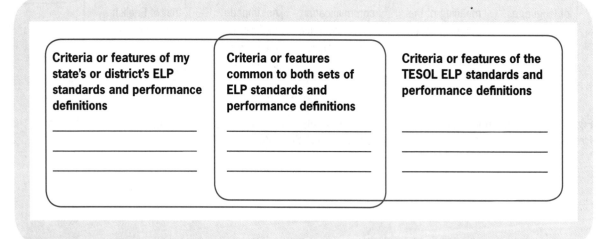

Criteria or features of my state's or district's ELP standards and performance definitions

_____
_____
_____

Criteria or features common to both sets of ELP standards and performance definitions

_____
_____
_____

Criteria or features of the TESOL ELP standards and performance definitions

_____
_____
_____

Figure 3.2. Comparison Between a State's or District's ELP Standards and Performance Definitions and the TESOL ELP Standards and Performance Definitions.

Task 3.3. Comparison of the TESOL Performance Definitions and English Language Proficiency Standards With Local Criteria and Standards

How do the TESOL performance definitions relate to the definitions used in your school district or state? Are the criteria similar for each language proficiency level? How do your district's or state's English language development standards compare with the TESOL ELP standards?

Use a Venn diagram like the one in Figure 3.2 to compare the criteria of the two sets of performance definitions and the features of the two sets of standards. Then summarize broad areas of similarities and differences.

Lila realized that there was not a strong correspondence between the criteria of the two sets of performance definitions. In addition, her state's English language development standards had six levels of English language proficiency, whereas the TESOL standards had five levels. To resolve these differences, she thought of a strategy to use as a professional development activity with the teachers in her district.

First, the language teachers teamed with content teachers and administrators by grade-level cluster. With Lila facilitating the process, teams decided on a number of language proficiency levels and their descriptive designations. Each team presented the rationale for its choice, and discussion ensued until consensus was reached by the whole group.

Next, each team was divided in half. One half was assigned the state's performance definitions, while the other half worked with the TESOL definitions. Using the worksheet in Figure 3.3, each team then collaborated to

A: *Agree on the most important criteria across the language proficiency levels*

E: *Examine the other group's selection of criteria*

I: *Integrate the two sets of criteria through discussion*

O: *Offer suggestions or recommendations, with justification, for the final set of criteria to constitute the performance definitions*

U: *Understand the value and use of the performance definitions to guide standards-based curriculum, instruction, and assessment for English language learners*

In the end, the whole group had ownership in the reconfiguration of the performance definitions. Later, Lila would share strategies for using these performance definitions with all teachers working with English language learners

My State's or District's Criteria	TESOL's Criteria	Combined Criteria

Figure 3.3. Creating Criteria for Performance Definitions for ELP Standards at a State or District Level.

in her district. At the next professional development opportunity, she planned to repeat the activity—with the goal of having the grade-level-cluster teams reach agreement on the features of ELP standards.

➤ How are the components of the TESOL English language proficiency standards organized?

The standards are organized by grade-level cluster (preK–K, 1–3, 4–5, 6–8, and 9–12) into matrices that are intended for classroom use. Each grade-level cluster has five matrices: one for each of the five standards. Every matrix consists of the following components:

- frame of native languages and cultures
- five levels of English language proficiency
- four language domains
- content topics
- strands of sample performance indicators

The 25 standards matrices appear in *PreK–12 English Language Proficiency Standards* (TESOL, 2006, pp. 48–97). As an example, Figure 3.4 reprints the listening and speaking domain sections of the matrix for Standard 1 (social, intercultural, and instructional language) at grade-level cluster 1–3. A blank matrix for individual or professional development use can be found in Appendix B.

Standard 1

English language learners **communicate** for SOCIAL, INTERCULTURAL, and INSTRUCTIONAL purposes within the school setting

Domain	Topic	Level 1	Level 2	Level 3	Level 4	Level 5
LISTENING	Directions Instructions	Mimic responses to one-step oral commands supported by gestures, songs, or realia	Follow one- to two-step oral commands supported by gestures, songs, or realia	Follow a series of oral commands supported by gestures, songs, or realia	Follow multistep commands within oral discourse supported by gestures or realia	Follow multistep commands within oral discourse in various contexts
SPEAKING	Feelings Emotions Needs	Respond to everyday oral requests or questions from a partner	Make requests, ask questions, or state reactions to everyday events, situations, or cultural experiences with a partner	Describe or recount reactions to everyday events, situations, or cultural experiences in small groups	Elaborate, using details or examples, reactions to events, situations, or cultural experiences	Present skits reflecting reactions to events, situations, or cultural experiences

NATIVE LANGUAGES & CULTURES

Figure 3.4. Listening and Speaking Domain Sections of the Matrix for ELP Standard 1, Grade-Level Cluster 1–3. Reprinted from *PreK–12 English Language Proficiency Standards* (TESOL, 2006, p. 58).

The TESOL standards matrix (adapted from that of the World-Class Instructional Design and Assessment Consortium, 2004) is formed by five levels of language proficiency along a horizontal axis and four language domains (listening, speaking, reading, and writing) along a vertical one. It is intended to stimulate instruction that is differentiated by language proficiency level and to be used as a tool for monitoring students' English language development throughout the school year. Through observation, interaction, or samples of student work, teachers can document how students perform on standards-based activities, tasks, or projects by language proficiency level in each language domain. In addition, the levels of language proficiency provide a convenient means for teachers to communicate with each other and to offer students coordinated, well-articulated instruction and feedback on their performance. The following sections describe each component of the standards matrix.

Native languages and cultures

Native languages and cultures provide a foundation for the standards matrix. Using native languages and cultures as a frame for teaching and learning reminds teachers and administrators to

- honor every student's linguistic and cultural heritage

- showcase students' linguistic and cultural heritages throughout the school and district

- recognize and build upon students' linguistic, cultural, and educational experiences as the backdrop and springboard for learning

- incorporate linguistic and cultural diversity into curriculum, instruction, and assessment

- allow students to use their native languages to facilitate English language development

English language learners' native languages and cultures are foundational for their academic achievement. As stated in the sixth principle of language proficiency (see Figure 2.1), students' proficiency in their native languages—in particular, their literacy—facilitates their acquisition of academic language proficiency in English. Irrespective of whether instruction is in the students' native languages or in English, teachers need to bring their students' languages, cultures, and life experiences into the classroom.

Task 3.4. Native Languages and Cultures

Think about ways to capitalize on your students' native languages and cultures in developing curriculum and instruction.

- How could you use the students' native languages and cultures as capital?

- How could you incorporate the students' native languages and cultures into your instructional assessment strategies?

- What kinds of native language resources, both inside and outside of school, are available to you and your students?

Paper to Practice: Using the TESOL English Language Proficiency Standards in PreK–12 Classrooms

Levels of English language proficiency

Within each matrix, English language proficiency is described along a continuum divided into five levels: Starting, Emerging, Developing, Expanding, and Bridging. These levels

- delineate language expectations for English language learners
- assume increasing linguistic complexity and increased length of utterance or processing of language
- presuppose vocabulary use from general to specialized to technical terms and expressions
- scaffold or build on each other
- provide examples of how students process or produce language within a language domain

Language domains

The four language domains—listening, speaking, reading, and writing—are presented independently to ensure that students

- have opportunities to process and practice their new language
- acquire both oral language and literacy in English
- use oral language to facilitate and reinforce literacy acquisition
- process and use language for specific purposes and contexts
- are exposed to language through content
- are afforded the use of multiple modalities to maximize understanding

Language domains are oftentimes combined during classroom instruction. In thematic units of instruction, for example, teachers use a unified topic to design oral language or literacy tasks across the content areas or standards. In everyday interaction, teachers ask questions while students answer, or teachers ask students to read a passage and respond in writing.

However, it is sometimes useful to approach the language domains separately in the classroom, especially for assessment. First, different students develop skills in different language domains at different rates. Therefore, it is important for teachers to have an understanding of their students' language profiles; that is, their performance in each language domain (Gottlieb & Hamayan, 2007). Second, the separation of language domains mirrors most state assessments of English language proficiency.

Content topics

Suggested content topics, drawn from the academic content standards of various states and national organizations, highlight the content or context for the strands of sample performance indicators across the five levels of English language proficiency for a given language domain.

Within the standards matrix, the column of suggested topics for each language domain and grade-level cluster helps teachers working with English language learners to

- organize and align standards-referenced curriculum

- integrate language and content in delivering instruction

- create multilevel lessons or units around a common theme

- share language education and content-based education practices

- provide a context for language instruction and assessment

The complete list of content topics from *PreK–12 English Language Proficiency Standards* (TESOL, 2006, pp. 142–147) is reprinted in Appendix A.

Strands of sample performance indicators

The strands of sample performance indicators (SPIs) contain the information that shapes instruction and assessment of English language learners according to the students' levels of English language proficiency. Each strand consists of all five levels of English language proficiency, represents a language domain within a standard, and is unified thematically through a sample topic derived from state academic content standards within the grade-level cluster. Within the strand, each language proficiency level builds upon the previous one, offering a cohesive flow to the language development process as students move across the continuum.

The strands of SPIs are the backbone of the TESOL English language proficiency standards. As suggested sequences of language development, strands of SPIs may be useful for

- embedding within existing curriculum or using as a springboard to design curriculum and units of study

- developing language and content objectives for lessons and units

- providing ideas for instructional assessment activities, tasks, and projects

- differentiating instruction and assessment by levels of English language proficiency

- documenting the language growth of English language learners over time

Figure 3.5 is an example of a strand taken from ELP Standard 4, the language of science, at the preK–K level.

The TESOL English language proficiency standards and their strands of SPIs are an expression of social, intercultural, and academic language designed for educators of English language learners. The performance definitions, with their common set of criteria for the five levels of English language proficiency, are a complement to the English language proficiency standards and the strands of SPIs. Figure 3.6 distinguishes the features of the performance definitions from those of the strands of SPIs.

Standard 4: The language of science
Grade-level cluster: PreK–K
Language domain: Speaking
Topic: Seasons and Weather

Level 1	Level 2	Level 3	Level 4	Level 5
Name realia or pictures associated with various times of the year (e.g., clothing, food)	Describe seasonal activities in home country or the United States from illustrations (and L1 support)	Answer *wh-* questions about photos or illustrations of different seasons or weather	Contrast characteristics of seasons or weather using photos or illustrations	Discuss likes and dislikes about seasons or weather

Figure 3.5. A Strand of Sample Performance Indicators From ELP Standard 4 (Topic: Seasons and Weather). Adapted from *PreK–12 English Language Proficiency Standards* (TESOL, 2006, p. 54).

	Standards-Referenced Features
Performance Definitions	• summarize criteria *across* the English language proficiency standards • describe second language (L2) development, preK through Grade 12, according to *levels of language proficiency* across the ELP standards and language domains
Strands of Sample Performance Indicators	• exemplify the progressive stages of language development *within* the standards matrix • use *grade-level-cluster topics* that provide the context for language presented by *standard, language domain,* and *language proficiency level*

Figure 3.6. Distinguishing Features of Performance Definitions and Strands of Sample Performance Indicators.

The sample performance indicators (SPIs) are the smallest unit of the English language proficiency standards matrix; an individual SPI represents a single cell within a strand. Each SPI contains three elements:

- a *language function*: how students use language to communicate

- *content*, exemplified in the *topic* for the specified standard: the context of the linguistic interaction

- *visual, graphic, or interactive supports*: how the language is reinforced through multiple modalities (Note: At Language Proficiency Level 5, few supports remain.)

These three essential elements are labeled in the sample performance indicator in Figure 3.7 and then further discussed. Chapter 4 provides a more thorough treatment of each element of an SPI and its potential contribution to curriculum, instruction, and assessment.

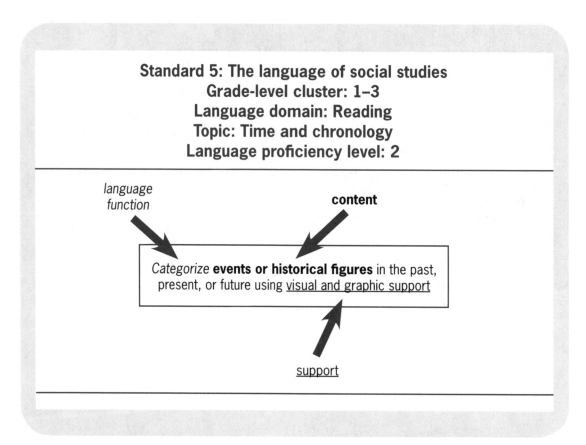

Figure 3.7. The Three Elements of a Sample Performance Indicator. Adapted from *PreK–12 English Language Proficiency Standards* (TESOL, 2006, p. 43).

Language functions

Sample performance indicators (SPIs) are introduced with language functions as their first element. Language functions should not be viewed in isolation; they work in conjunction with given topics or content (as noted by the standard), the language domain, and forms of support. In addition, language functions are closely related to the language structures—grammar, vocabulary, and discourse—and the language registers required at a given level of language proficiency within a grade-level cluster.

Language functions communicate the intent of a message; in a way, they direct students to process or use language for a specific purpose. The individual English language proficiency standards provide the larger context in which the language functions operate. When approaching a language function, consider what language is necessary at this level of English language proficiency for English language learners to *compare*, *analyze*, *critique*, and so on (Gottlieb, Cranley, & Oliver, 2007).

Bloom's taxonomy of cognitive functions (1956) cannot be interchanged with the specific language demands included in a sample performance indicator, nor can it be superimposed onto the levels of English language proficiency across a strand. As stated in the second principle of language proficiency (see Figure 2.1), under the right conditions, complex thinking can be expressed in relatively simple language. For example, the SPI in Figure 3.7 includes the language function *categorize*. This function involves high-level thinking that requires analysis, yet it is present at Language Proficiency Level 2, when English language proficiency is at an Emerging stage.

In the sample performance indicator in Figure 3.7, young English language learners may initially engage in a cognitively complex activity while given supports for language learning within a familiar context, such as categorizing the stages of their personal development. They might learn through hands-on activities that *categorizing* means putting pictures or objects into different groups or sorting by a given feature or characteristic. They may use language such as "I put this here" or "I put that there" to express their understanding of how to categorize.

With further instruction and a graphic organizer, such as a three-column chart with the labels *Past*, *Present*, and *Future*, the students can be expected to read labeled illustrations and sort them according to their temporal status. Having gained familiarity with the graphic organizer as a means of support, the students may then delve into more unfamiliar territory, such as categorizing events related to their community, city, or state.

Although the same language functions can occur across grade-level clusters, standards, language domains, and levels of language proficiency, the language demands may vary. In Figure 3.8, the language function *compare* is used across three contiguous levels of language proficiency, from Level 2 through Level 4. The language demand of the context (stipulated by the language proficiency level as outlined in the performance definitions) progressively increases as students move from comparing familiar, concrete characteristics using general vocabulary to comparing unfamiliar, abstract ideas requiring more detail, specialized language, and specific discourse structures.

Standard 2: The language of language arts
Grade-level cluster: 4–5
Language domain: Speaking
Topic: Point of view

Level 2	Level 3	Level 4
Compare physical traits of self or others with pictures of familiar persons	*Compare* physical traits of self with graphic depictions of characters in familiar fiction	*Compare*/contrast character traits or points of view of self with those of characters in fiction

Figure 3.8. The Use of the Same Language Function Across Levels of English Language Proficiency. Adapted from *PreK–12 English Language Proficiency Standards* (TESOL, 2006, p. 70).

Task 3.5. Language Functions

In general, language functions may serve social or academic purposes, depending on their context. Examine the ELP standards matrix for a grade-level cluster with which you are familiar. Refer to *PreK–12 English Language Proficiency Standards* (TESOL, 2006, pp. 48–97) or to your state's ELP standards.

1. Use a chart like the one below to categorize some of the language functions according to their use: Are they social (e.g., *apologize* to a peer) or academic (e.g., *summarize* experiments)—or can they be used in both contexts (e.g., *describe* a friend vs. *describe* the Ming Dynasty)?

2. List the language functions within the SPIs that involve high levels of cognitive engagement at lower levels of English language proficiency.

Purposes of Language Functions		
Social Uses	**Academic Uses**	**Both Social and Academic Uses**
Examples of Sample Performance Indicators That Involve High Levels of Cognitive Engagement at Lower Levels of English Language Proficiency	
Language Functions Within Sample Performance Indicators	**Levels of English Language Proficiency**

Content topics

Each sample performance indicator guides teachers in presenting the language requisite for students to meet the specified ELP standard by referring to content material on a grade-level-appropriate topic. The topics come from the list of content topics in Appendix A. The topics in this list are organized by grade-level cluster and drawn from the academic content standards of multiple states and national organizations. As previously mentioned, this list of topics first appeared in *PreK–12 English Language Proficiency Standards* (TESOL, 2006, pp. 142–147). The topics are generally broad in scope, to maximize their representation across states, districts, and language education programs. As students move across the grade-level clusters, the topics spiral to represent more in-depth coverage, just as curriculum does.

Task 3.6. Content Topics

The list of content topics in Appendix A offers a variety of the range of academic topics that provide the backdrop for language development within each grade-level cluster. Review the topics for one or more English language proficiency standards within a grade-level cluster that is familiar to you.

Select one grade within the cluster. As you examine the content topics, categorize them into three groups using the chart below: topics that match what is taught at that grade in your school or program, topics that are related to what is taught at that grade in your school or program, and topics that are not addressed at that grade in your school or program.

Compare your results with those of a colleague who teaches the grade you selected. You may wish to add topics from your curriculum not on the list.

Grade: _____	Topics That Match Our Curriculum	Topics That Relate to Our Curriculum	Topics Not Included in Our Curriculum
Standard 1: Social, intercultural, and instructional language			
Standard 2: The language of language arts			
Standard 3: The language of mathematics			
Standard 4: The language of science			
Standard 5: The language of social studies			

Because classroom and content teachers hold the key to the academic language of their content areas, the topics are a good starting point for their collaboration with language teachers. Language teachers may, for example, show grade-level teachers how to use Standard 1 (social, intercultural, and instructional language) to tap students' prior experiences and cross-cultural understanding as the entrée into content-area topics.

Instructional supports

The sample performance indicators (SPIs) for the TESOL English language proficiency standards rely on three different forms of support: visual, graphic, and interactive. Although useful for all students, instructional supports are critical for English language learners to access content through language. Some form of support is present in each strand of SPIs through ELP Level 4. Students at Level 5, like their English-proficient peers, generally do not require such supports. A list of common instructional supports can be found in Figure 4.9.

Visual supports, such as gestures, manipulatives, diagrams, or video clips, reinforce ideas presented orally or in writing. Graphic supports, such as charts, tables, or graphic organizers, provide ways to organize information so it becomes more comprehensible. Interactive supports, such as working in cooperative groups or with partners, accessing technology, or using their native language, afford English language learners opportunities to practice their new language with others, conduct research, and clarify or confirm the intent of a communication. The use of supports readily extends to formative assessment, in which classroom teachers measure students' mastery of the language objectives of a lesson.

Interaction among the elements of the sample performance indicators

Many language functions in the strands of sample performance indicators (e.g., *sequence*, *sort*, or *compare*) can be found across a range of language proficiency levels, language domains, standards, and grade-level clusters. Implicit is the notion that both young English language learners and students at the lower levels of English language proficiency can engage in higher level thinking, given the needed support and within the expectations of the language proficiency level. The specific language required of the language function within a sample performance indicator therefore depends on a student's age, his or her level of English language proficiency, the context of interaction (as dictated by the English language proficiency standard), and the language targets set by teachers. *Language target* is a general term that refers to a variety of possible language features, some of which may become language objectives in planning a specific lesson or unit of instruction.

Students can deal with cognitively demanding tasks when language is made comprehensible for specific levels of English language proficiency and when grade-level content is supported visually, graphically, or interactively. The second principle of language proficiency states that language proficiency can reflect complex thinking when linguistic complexity is reduced and support is present (see Figure 2.1). This principle is illustrated in Figure 3.9.

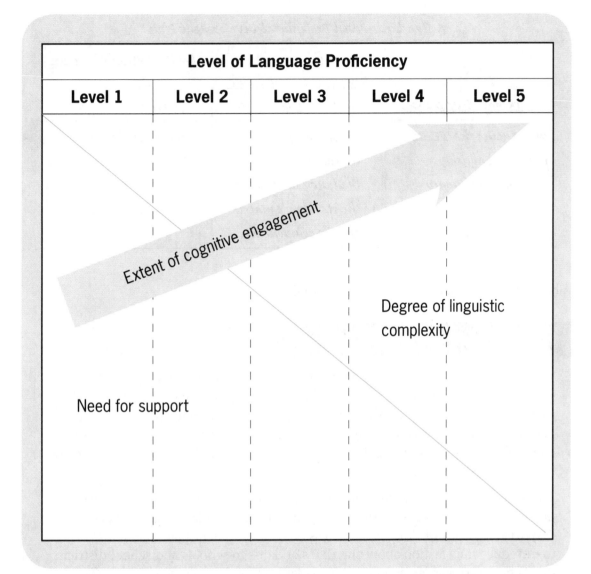

Level of Language Proficiency

| Level 1 | Level 2 | Level 3 | Level 4 | Level 5 |

Extent of cognitive engagement

Degree of linguistic complexity

Need for support

Figure 3.9. High Levels of Cognitive Engagement Superimposed Across the Levels of Language Proficiency. Adapted from *PreK–12 English Language Proficiency Standards* (TESOL, 2006, p. 106).

Thus, all three elements of an SPI work together to delineate how language is used in a particular situation. The strands of SPIs serve as the stimuli for teachers to identify the language associated with a given language function within a specified context.

Lila had so much information about the English language proficiency standards to share with teachers and building administrators that she decided to organize, with the help of the district coordinators, a professional development plan for the school year. She wanted to ensure that there would be sustained, open dialogue in the district on the growing school population of English language learners and on the effective use of standards-based education. Her first step was to begin sketching out the following chart:

A Standards-Based Professional Development Plan		
Workshop/Course Topic	_Description or Objectives of Workshop/Course_	_Participants, Dates, and Duration (in hours or days)_
introducing the TESOL preK–12 English language proficiency standards	• _rationale for the standards_ • _the language of school_ • _the standards matrix and its components_	• _grade-level teams of language, content, and classroom teachers_ • _half-day workshop_

A blank version of Lila's chart appears in Appendix C.

Reflect and Respond

This chapter reviews the components of the TESOL English language proficiency standards within the matrix format and further discusses the strands and elements of the sample performance indicators. In addition, it shows how the performance definitions work alongside the ELP standards to help educators gain a comprehensive picture of English language learners at each language milestone or level of English language proficiency.

Think about how you can use the information related to the standards matrix and impart it to other teachers with whom you share English language learners. You may wish to begin working on a professional development plan that shows how to introduce information about the ELP standards to schools and school districts throughout the year. As you do so, consider each of the following:

- the criteria and role of the performance definitions

- the presentation of the standards matrix framework and its components

- the shared uses for strands of sample performance indicators among teachers

Use the template in Appendix C and add workshop topics as you read through the chapters of _Paper to Practice_.

Vignette Revisited

Lila understood that every teacher was a language teacher who needed to become familiar with the TESOL English language proficiency standards so that English language learners could successfully access the language of school. Because she had English language learners across several schools and three grade-level clusters (preK–K, 1–3, and 4–5), Lila realized that she must share information about the ELP standards with the many other teachers who worked with these students. As a starting point, Lila decided that for each English language learner she would color code the performance definitions by the student's level of English language proficiency and discuss the student's individual language expectations with his or her teachers.

Personally, Lila intended to use the ELP standards as a tool for planning instruction and assessment for English language learners. Each month she would introduce different standards and strands of sample performance indicators. As a coach, she would model their use in various classrooms. Thinking ahead, she might even use the standards matrix to monitor individual student progress in language development throughout the school year.

Chapter 4
Expanding the Usefulness of the Strands of Sample Performance Indicators

One of the beauties of teaching is that there is no limit to one's growth as a teacher, just as there is no knowing beforehand how much your students can learn.

—Herbert Kohl

Guiding Question

➤ **How can each element of the sample performance indicators be used to develop a deeper understanding of academic language?**

Vignette

At a recent district in-service workshop, Gordon Vann had been introduced to the TESOL English language proficiency (ELP) standards. As a 10th-grade English teacher with a number of English language learners in his classes, Gordon recognized that the standards could help him provide more individualized instruction for learners at various levels of English language proficiency. As he reviewed the component parts of the strands of sample performance indicators (SPIs), he began to think about how he could expand their usefulness. After all, there was only one standards matrix, across four language domains, that was relevant to his classroom. How could he build on it to develop language targets that would enhance his lesson planning?

The strands of sample performance indicators illustrate the range of instructional practices that must be crafted to provide access to academic language and content to students at varying language proficiency levels. As discussed in chapter 3, each SPI within those strands contains three main elements:

- a *language function*, or how students use language to communicate

- a content-related *topic* for the specified standard

- visual, graphic, or interactive *supports* that exemplify how the language is reinforced (at Language Proficiency Levels 1–4)

Although we discuss them individually, in practice the elements are linked during classroom instruction. For teachers like Gordon Vann, these components can act as entry points for designing instruction that is appropriate to a wide range of classrooms and student needs.

> ## ➤ How can each element of the sample performance indicators be used to develop a deeper understanding of academic language?

In the following sections, we examine each of the three elements of a sample performance indicator in more detail to support the development of language targets for student learning. We use the term *language targets* to refer to a range of possible language features that may become language objectives. We use the term *language objectives* when those features are tied to specific lesson plans.

Language functions

In working with the language functions, educators need to determine what language is associated with each function in meaningful communication. Figure 4.1 shows a range of sample language functions for each language domain, drawn from the ELP standards matrices. Keep in mind while reviewing this table that many language functions may apply to more than one language domain. For example, students can *describe* people or places when they speak and when they write; they may *interpret* information when listening or reading. Grade level also affects how a language function operates and how it is expressed at a particular language proficiency level.

LISTENING
• follow oral directions or commands
• identify sounds, words, phrases, objects, figures, features, or places
• role-play or dramatize scenes or activities
• sequence events, processes, or procedures
• create or organize displays, models, or murals

SPEAKING
• describe people, places, events, phenomena, or processes
• explain relationships
• present information, reviews, or reports
• debate issues or take stances
• discuss and give examples of uses, functions, or properties

READING
• categorize pictures, phrases, sentences, or paragraphs
• interpret information or results
• match pictures with words, phrases, sentences, or paragraphs
• draw conclusions or infer from sentences, paragraphs, or research materials
• order, rank, or sequence phrases, sentences, and paragraphs

WRITING
• list, classify, or categorize features, traits, locations, or preferences
• compare and contrast features, traits, locations, or preferences
• summarize personal experiences, information, and narrative or expository text
• narrate stories, events, procedures, or processes
• compose essays, reports, reviews, or critiques

Figure 4.1. Sample Language Functions Across Language Domains and English Language Proficiency Standards.

Task 4.1. Language Functions

Using Figure 4.1 as a reference, create your own list of language functions and potential activities or tasks for a grade level and content area that are pertinent to your own teaching context. Use the chart below to record your ideas.

Example:

Grade: _____2_____

Content Area: _____language arts_____

Language Domain: _____listening_____

Language Function: _____identify_____

Activity: _____story elements in fairy tales_____

Grade or Grade-Level Cluster: _____
Content Area: _____
LISTENING Language Functions and Activities
SPEAKING Language Functions and Activities
READING Language Functions and Activities
WRITING Language Functions and Activities

Common Language Functions Across Standards	Related Language Functions
categorize	classify, group, sort
compare	contrast, differentiate, distinguish
connect	apply, associate, find relationships, link, match
create	compose, illustrate, produce, synthesize
describe	give examples, relate, tell about
discuss	elaborate, explain, provide reasons
evaluate	defend, interpret, judge, make choices
identify	find, indicate, label, locate, name, point to, select
imagine	adapt, design, estimate, hypothesize, predict, project
sequence	arrange, order, outline, rank, trace steps

Figure 4.2. A Categorization Scheme of Related Language Functions.

Exploring related functions can extend the range of the language functions found in the strands of sample performance indicators. The list of common language functions in Figure 4.2 has been compiled from the TESOL ELP standards matrices.

For a project about advertising in the print media, Gordon's students would be making group presentations about their analyses of persuasive elements in magazine ads. In their presentations, his students would describe the elements as well as their appeal. As Gordon considered the language that students would use during this task, he thought about the language functions related to persuasion. Starting with persuade, he jotted down some functions that his students might find useful in their talks:

persuade: manipulate, influence, convince, offer, sway, win over

Task 4.2. Related Language Functions

Choose a language function appropriate to your classroom context. Use the graphic organizer below to brainstorm related language functions. You might want to think about a specific ELP standard or combination of standards in creating your set of related language functions.

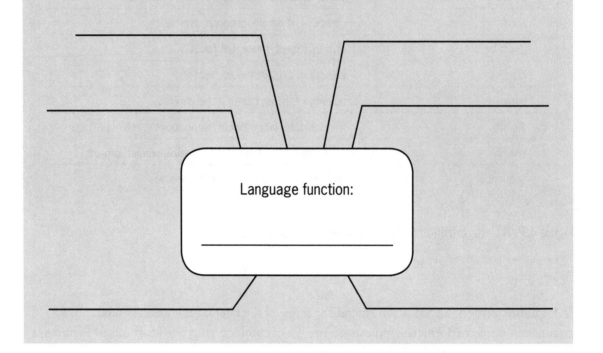

The first step in using language functions for planning instruction is to identify typical language patterns associated with those functions at each English language proficiency level. Although many linguistic options can be associated with a specified language function, some suggestions are found in Figure 4.3. As the table shows, the target language varies by language proficiency level; however, teachers must also consider grade level and content area when deciding which language patterns to teach.

Language Function	Examples of Language Patterns by Language Proficiency Level				
	Level 1	Level 2	Level 3	Level 4	Level 5
categorize or sort pictures, phrases, sentences, paragraphs	this/that these/those	This/that goes here. These/those go there.	This group has ___. That group has ___.	Although this group has ___, that group has ___.	Inasmuch as this group consists of ___, that group ___.
compare and contrast features, traits, locations, preferences	same/different	the same as/ different from	just like/is similar to One is ___er, but the other is the ___est.	in the same way/instead of	similarly on the other hand/in contrast to
describe people, places, events, phenomena, processes	It's ___. They're ___.	all, most, many, some	almost all, mostly, a few, several	usually, often, once in a while	generally, occasionally, rarely
interpret information, results	more/less	There are greater/fewer ___ than ___.	There seems to be ___.	The fact that there are ___ means that ___.	The data show that ___; therefore, ___.
predict outcomes		I think . . .	I believe that . . .	It is my opinion that . . .	I would suggest/ predict that . . .
sequence a series	one, two, three	first, second, third	beginning, middle, end before, now, after	on, next, then, finally	initially, subsequently, lastly
show cause and effect		because	If ___, then ___.	In order to . . . so	as a result consequently

Figure 4.3. Suggested Language Patterns Associated With Language Functions by Language Proficiency Level.

Task 4.3. Language Patterns

Consider how you might use the language function element of the sample performance indicators to identify language targets for your students. Begin by browsing through the standards matrices in *PreK–12 English Language Proficiency Standards* (TESOL, 2006) or the example matrices in this volume. You may also use your state's English language proficiency standards as a resource.

Look carefully at the strands of sample performance indicators at a grade-level cluster appropriate to your setting. Consider your students' levels of English language proficiency. Then use the material in Figure 4.3 to help you identify some language patterns students need to learn in order to perform the learning tasks for one or more of the language domains. List these language patterns in the table.

Language Function	Some Language Patterns by Language Proficiency Level				
	Level 1	Level 2	Level 3	Level 4	Level 5

Content topics

Appendix A provides lists of content topics derived from national and state academic content standards. These topics are generally broad in scope and are developed in greater depth as students move across the grade-level clusters. Figure 4.4 provides a sampling of common topics addressed in the strands of SPIs for each English language proficiency standard across grade-level clusters.

Each topic may consist of many subtopics that are specific to states, districts, schools, or classrooms. Both the broader topics and their subtopics represent academic content standards. Topics and subtopics generally spiral from grade level to grade level. Figure 4.5 provides examples of the potential breakdown of topics into subtopics that are applicable for each grade-level cluster and ELP standard.

Standard 1: Social, Intercultural, and Instructional Language	Standard 2: The Language of Language Arts	Standard 3: The Language of Mathematics	Standard 4: The Language of Science	Standard 5: The Language of Social Studies
feelings and emotions	main idea and details	basic number operations	animals	forms of government
interpersonal misunderstandings	phonemic awareness/ morphology	data	change	historical events, figures, and leaders
likes, dislikes, and preferences	point of view	estimation	cycles	maps
school life	story grammar	patterns	ecology	revolution
strategies		shapes	living systems	rights and responsibilities
traditions and values		units of measurement	plants	
			processes	
			weather	

Figure 4.4. Examples of Standards-Based Topics Across Grade-Level Clusters.

ELP STANDARD	Example Topic	Ideas for Subtopics				
		PreK–K	1–3	4–5	6–8	9–12
1	school life	classroom routines	people and their jobs	preferred activities	social interaction	extracurricular activities
2	points of view	self and family	familiar people	character perspective	author perspective	genre perspective
3	estimation	sizes	large whole numbers	prices and cost (with tax)	mean (averages)	conditional probability
4	animals	farm and zoo	mammals, reptiles, and amphibians	prehistoric, vertebrates and invertebrates	one-celled, multi-celled	taxonomies, species
5	maps	our classroom	our school, neighborhood, and community	product and topographical	aerial, features, properties, symbols	historical, projections

Figure 4.5. Examples of the Breakdown of Topics Into Subtopics by Grade-Level Cluster From the Five ELP Standards.

Topics may also be combined across standards to provide students with more in-depth coverage. Because Standard 1 (social, intercultural, and instructional language) can be directly connected to students' everyday experiences, a teacher may introduce a topic through this familiar venue to build background knowledge before launching into the more specialized content-based topic. Teachers may also use multiple standards to create a thematic unit of instruction with an extended project that integrates more than one language domain.

Gordon realized that the genres generally studied in a 10th-grade English class might challenge some of his English language learners. Therefore, he would try to connect them to his students' prior experiences. He was slated to begin a unit of study on autobiographical and biographical narratives, a topic listed in the standards matrix under Standard 2, the language of language arts (see Figure 4.6). Gordon looked at the topics listed in the matrix for Standard 1 (social, intercultural, and instructional language) and chose Misunderstandings from the Speaking domain (see Figure 4.7). Gordon felt that the student talk in the activities for this topic would prepare his students to develop more thoughtful and reflective personal written narratives.

Standard 2: The language of language arts
Grade-level cluster: 9–12
Language domain: Writing
Topic: Autobiographical and biographical narratives

Level 1	Level 2	Level 3	Level 4	Level 5
Label personal photographs, artifacts, or drawings with words or phrases	List life events sequentially or along a time line using phrases or short sentences	Summarize life events organized by time period using personal resources (e.g., albums, birth certificates)	Create personal essays using as models familiar autobiographies or memoirs read (in L1 or L2)	Compose autobiographical essays or memoirs

Figure 4.6. A Strand of Sample Performance Indicators From ELP Standard 2 (Topic: Autobiographical and Biographical Narratives). Adapted from *PreK–12 English Language Proficiency Standards* (TESOL, 2006, p. 91).

Standard 1: Social, intercultural, and instructional language
Grade-level cluster: 9–12
Language domain: Speaking
Topic: Misunderstandings

Level 1	Level 2	Level 3	Level 4	Level 5
Share potential cross-cultural misunderstandings in small groups (using L1)	Give examples of cross-cultural misunderstandings in small groups (confirming through L1)	Present and pose solutions to cross-cultural misunderstandings in small groups or with a partner	Negotiate solutions to resolve cross-cultural misunderstandings with a partner	Offer suggestions and guidance on how to reach compromise or agreement on cross-cultural misunderstandings

Figure 4.7. A Strand of Sample Performance Indicators From ELP Standard 1 (Topic: Misunderstandings). Adapted from *PreK–12 English Language Proficiency Standards* (TESOL, 2006, p. 88).

Whereas language functions provide insight into general language patterns students need to learn, topics help to identify other language targets, such as key vocabulary and discourse structures that may be used to teach or learn about an academic subject. For example, Figure 4.5 shows examples of subtopics for the topic of animals in Standard 4, the language of science. Figure 4.8 illustrates how these subtopics can be elaborated upon to identify possible language targets at each grade-level cluster. Consider two examples of vocabulary and discourse associated with these subtopics:

- In a kindergarten class focusing on farm animals and their habitats, students may see a range of illustrated words to identify farmyard animals. They may also learn about the animals' characteristics and environments through picture books, songs, or role-playing.

- In a biology lesson on the kinds of cells, high school students learn new terms, definitions, and characteristics. They listen to the teacher's explanations of these terms and learn how to apply them in academic discourse genres such as lab reports and research papers.

Topic: Animals	PreK–K	1–3	4–5	6–8	9–12
Subtopic	farm and zoo	mammals, reptiles, and amphibians	prehistoric, vertebrates and invertebrates	one-celled, multi-celled	taxonomies, species
Vocabulary	cow, pig, lion	animal features adaptation habitat	fossil record geologic evidence extinction	cell fundamental unit of life unicellular, multicellular	hierarchical classification DNA sequence phylogenetics
Discourse Structures / Genres	narrative rhyme	story expository text	textbooks	lab report	Cornell notes lab report research paper

Figure 4.8. Examples of Language Targets by Topic Across Grade-Level Clusters.

Task 4.4. Subtopics and Language Targets

Review the materials or curriculum your English language learners are using in one of their content areas. What content topics are your students learning about? Now look through the standards matrices in *PreK–12 English Language Proficiency Standards* (TESOL, 2006) or the example matrices in this volume for topics or subtopics similar to those your students are studying. You may also use your state's English language proficiency standards as a resource. Use the information from one sample performance indicator as a starting point to fill in the chart below with language targets tied to the topic or subtopic.

Grade-Level Content Topic:	Subtopic:
Key Vocabulary:	
Discourse Structures / Genres:	

Instructional supports

The English language proficiency standards rely on three forms of support in their strands of sample performance indicators. The supports are critical for all but the highest level English language learners to access content through language and are thus included through ELP Level 4. *Visual supports* reinforce ideas presented orally or in writing, often with hands-on materials. *Graphic supports* provide ways to organize information so it becomes more comprehensible. Finally, *interactive supports* afford students opportunities to practice their new language with others, clarify or confirm the intent of a communication through their native language, or conduct research using the Internet. Figure 4.9 lists classroom examples of each of these forms of support.

Because all strands of sample performance indicators contain some form of support, they provide examples that can be used for planning lessons. They can also be shared with other colleagues who teach English language learners. Although supports can scaffold learning, teachers need to think through carefully how they will implement the support. Inviting students to work in groups, for example, requires advance planning to ensure that students know what to do and how to interact purposefully. Providing students with props or realia means preparing the materials ahead of time to have them available and ready to use at the appropriate time.

Visual Supports	
advertisements	models
artifacts	multimedia
bulletin boards	murals
cartoons	newspapers
diagrams	photographs
dramatization, role-plays	picture dictionaries
equipment and supplies (including content-specific materials)	pictures
	props
flash cards	realia/real-life objects
gestures	sign language
icons or symbols	SMART Boards™
illustrated books	software, Web sites
illustrations	tools (e.g., calculators, scales)
magazines	transparencies
manipulatives	TV, videos
maps and globes	word walls

Graphic Supports	
board games	graphs (e.g., bar graphs, line graphs)
charts (e.g., flowcharts, pie charts)	number lines
graphic organizers (e.g., T-charts, Venn diagrams, semantic webs)	tables
	time lines

Interactive Supports	
cooperative group structures	peers
field trips or class experiences	small groups or teams
mentors	teacher oral scaffolding
other adults (e.g., family members, paraprofessionals)	technology (e.g., computer)
	tutors
partners or pairs	use of native language

Figure 4.9. Examples of Visual, Graphic, and Interactive Supports.

After studying the SPIs for the TESOL English language proficiency standards, Gordon began to incorporate a variety of supports into his high school English class lessons. He provided bilingual dictionaries in the native languages of the students; when no bilingual dictionary was available, he made sure those students had first use of the computers on which native language resources had been bookmarked. During his lectures, he interspersed diagrams (to illustrate plot lines, for example) or made use of the overhead projector in his classroom. When students worked in groups, Gordon made a point of interacting with each group to provide verbal scaffolding as needed. He also encouraged students to exchange information with each other as a check for understanding. At first it was difficult for Gordon to integrate these supports into his teaching, but he soon found that all his students, not just his English language learners, were benefiting.

Task 4.5. Instructional Supports

Review the lists of supports in Figure 4.9. Enter those that you use on a regular basis in the chart below. Then add any additional supports that you find effective in working with English language learners.

Examine your chart. Which form of support (visual, graphic, or interactive) do you tend to rely on the most? Do you use multiple forms of support in planning your lessons?

Supports Used With English Language Learners		
Visual	**Graphic**	**Interactive**

In this chapter we have analyzed the three main elements found in every strand of sample performance indicators. This analysis is a starting point for thinking about how to use these elements in developing language targets related to content learning. The sample performance indicators, at the core of the ELP standards matrices, can be the basis for classroom instructional and assessment activities geared to specific language proficiency levels and grade-level clusters. In section II of this book, we look more specifically at how teachers can draw on the SPIs in their instructional and assessment planning.

Reflect and Respond

This chapter shows how each element of the sample performance indicators can help educators explore the language demands inherent in academic tasks across grades and language proficiency levels.

Think about how you might use the information in the SPIs to identify potential language targets related to the content lessons you teach. Consider each of the following:

- What topics do you cover? What subtopics?
- What language functions can you identify?
- What language patterns are associated with these functions?
- What language supports can you use to reinforce learning for students at each level of language proficiency?

Vignette Revisited

After experimenting with various elements of the SPIs, Gordon realized how useful they were in creating appropriate lessons for his students. To start a unit on persuasive writing techniques, he reviewed the standards and grade-level clusters relevant to his teaching context. After identifying a topic that matched his curriculum—Points of View, he considered ways of developing language targets for his students.

Gordon studied the language functions in the strand of SPIs for this topic and focused on the functions listed for ELP Levels 3 and 4, the levels represented by his English language learners. He wrote these functions on a piece of paper, along with several other language functions that would tie in with his persuasive writing unit. Then Gordon listed language features relevant to the identified functions, so he could incorporate them into his lesson plans. His notes for two of the language functions looked like this:

Language Functions	Language Features
Compare and contrast	This _____ is similar to / different from _____ because . . .
	By comparison,
	Just like . . .
	In contrast,
Draw conclusions	Based on . . .
	As a result of _____,

Finally, Gordon chose several supports to incorporate in the unit, keeping in mind the available resources and the time allocated for the unit. As Gordon reviewed his planning, he felt confident that his students would actively engage in learning academic language linked to the content of his persuasive writing unit.

Section II

How Can We Implement Standards-Based Instruction and Assessment?

Chapter 5
Promoting Standards-Based Education Through Collaboration

We will surely get to our destination if we join hands.

—Aung San Suu Kyi

Guiding Questions

➤ **How can educators work together on behalf of English language learners?**

➤ **How can school and district leaders stimulate collaboration?**

➤ **How can the TESOL English language proficiency standards foster collaboration among stakeholders?**

Vignette

Cam Nguyen, a technology and language arts teacher, led the humanities team at her large urban middle school. Her teammates were Michael Grant, the social studies teacher; Christine Patel, the language arts teacher; and Rachel Numan, the ESL teacher. Their community had a high percentage of English language learners. As a result, the entire K–12 district had adopted the TESOL English language proficiency (ELP) standards and systematically infused academic language development into the curriculum.

The teachers on the humanities team often combined forces to develop thematic units; they were currently exploring one on student identity, with a goal of building the adolescents' self-confidence and responsibility. The team members believed that the middle school students would benefit from being reading buddies to younger students. Fortunately, the middle school was adjacent to the feeder K–5 elementary school.

Cam initiated an after-school meeting of her team with the neighboring kindergarten teachers to suggest the idea of a literacy club. The kindergarten teachers were thrilled that the middle school students would become their young students' literacy buddies. Together the humanities team and the kindergarten teachers delved into their copies of PreK–12 English Language Proficiency Standards (TESOL, 2006) to select topics and strands of sample performance indicators (SPIs) to begin their Book Brigade.

The group agreed on two topics from the 6–8 grade-level cluster: Multiculturalism (from Standard 1: social, intercultural, and instructional language) and Cultural perspectives and frames of reference (from Standard 5: the language of social studies). These topics reflected the spiraling of curriculum from the earliest of grades and corresponded with the two topics the teachers selected from the preK–K grade-level cluster: Homes and habitats and Friends and family, both from Standard 5: the language of social studies. (The relevant strands of sample performance indicators for all four topics are reprinted in Figures 5.1–5.4.) To encourage the older students' active participation, they would be charged with selecting multicultural books about friends and families from the elementary school library.

Grade-level cluster: 6–8
Standard 1: Social, intercultural, and instructional language
Language domain: Reading
Topic: Multiculturalism

Level 1	Level 2	Level 3	Level 4	Level 5
Search for and identify topics of personal interest using illustrations (from L1, Internet, or newspapers)	Indicate preferences by rank-ordering or classifying illustrated topics of personal interest	Gather and sort illustrated information according to topics of interest or diverse perspectives	Arrange illustrated information from multiple, diverse sources in logical order	Create original displays of information (e.g., posters, graphic organizers, brochures) from multiple, diverse sources

Figure 5.1. A Strand of Sample Performance Indicators From ELP Standard 1 (Topic: Multiculturalism). Adapted from *PreK–12 English Language Proficiency Standards* (TESOL, 2006, p. 79).

Grade-level cluster: 6–8
Standard 5: The language of social studies
Language domain: Writing
Topic: Cultural perspectives and frames of reference

Level 1	Level 2	Level 3	Level 4	Level 5
List characteristics of people, places, or time periods using visual or graphic cultural references	Describe people, places, or time periods using visual or graphic cultural references (e.g., map of Southeast Asia or artifacts from Ming Dynasty)	Compare/contrast people, places, or time periods using visual or graphic cultural references (e.g., Aztec, Mayan, and Egyptian pyramids)	Give detailed examples of cross-cultural connections among people, places, or time periods using visual or graphic cultural references	Defend and provide support for cross-cultural perspectives

Figure 5.2. A Strand of Sample Performance Indicators From ELP Standard 5 (Topic: Cultural Perspectives and Frames of Reference). Adapted from *PreK–12 English Language Proficiency Standards* (TESOL, 2006, p. 87).

Grade-level cluster: PreK–K
Standard 5: The language of social studies
Language domain: Speaking
Topic: Homes and habitats

Level 1	Level 2	Level 3	Level 4	Level 5
Repeat names of different types of homes or habitats from pictures (e.g., nest, house)	Describe homes or habitats as part of rhymes, chants, and songs in a large group	Recite predictable sentence patterns that have visual support (e.g., "A bird lives in a nest.")	Compare different types of homes or habitats found in nonfiction picture books	Provide information on location and directionality of homes or habitats (e.g., ". . . up in a tree," ". . . next to my house")

Figure 5.3. A Strand of Sample Performance Indicators From ELP Standard 5 (Topic: Homes and Habitats). Adapted from *PreK–12 English Language Proficiency Standards* (TESOL, 2006, p. 56).

Grade-level cluster: PreK–K
Standard 5: The language of social studies
Language domain: Writing
Topic: Friends and family

Level 1	Level 2	Level 3	Level 4	Level 5
Draw pictures of shared experiences with a friend	Label pictures of self, friends, or family members using a combination of letters and scribble writings	Draw and label familiar people or places using pictures and a combination of scribble writing, letters, and words with invented spellings	Make illustrated lists of familiar people or places in pairs or triads using a combination of letters, words, and phrases with invented spellings	Create picture books or stories with a partner using a combination of words and phrases with invented spellings

Figure 5.4. A Strand of Sample Performance Indicators From ELP Standard 5 (Topic: Friends and Family). Adapted from *PreK–12 English Language Proficiency Standards* (TESOL, 2006, p. 57).

In this chapter, we explore collaborative avenues for teachers and school leaders serving English language learners. Collaboration among teachers working with English language learners may be a challenge, in some instances, or perhaps a painfully slow endeavor (Davison, 2006). However, we believe that the TESOL English language proficiency standards—coupled with team-based, ongoing professional development opportunities—empower all teachers to share the responsibility for educating second language learners.

➤ How can educators work together on behalf of English language learners?

Every day at school, English language learners come in contact with many different adult language models. Each one has a potential impact on the students' language development, whether in their native language or in English. Ultimately, in order for collaboration among these adults to take hold and flourish, a school culture must be rich and vibrant in its social and personal relationships (Lacina, Levine, & Sowa, 2006).

Irrespective of the instructional approaches found in a school or district, many teachers touch the lives of English language learners. As Figure 5.5 illustrates, we envision English language learners as the center of a flower, with their educators as the petals. Identifying the key players in the education of English language learners facilitates this student-centered perspective.

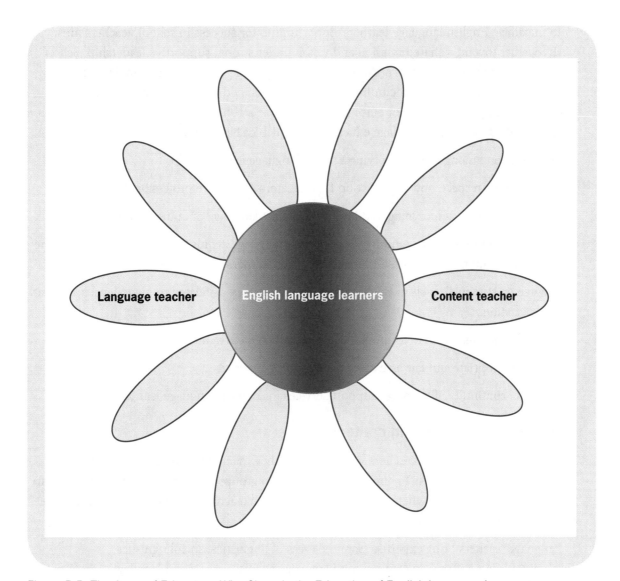

Figure 5.5. The Array of Educators Who Share in the Education of English Language Learners. Adapted from Gottlieb (2006, p. 4).

Task 5.1. Teachers Serving English Language Learners

Complete the flower in Figure 5.5 by writing down the educators who work with English language learners in your school, such as specialists (Title I or literacy coaches), classroom teachers, or specials (fine arts and physical education instructors).

What steps could you take to reach out to teachers who have English language learners in their classrooms but who may not have your experience or training in language education? (For example, to initiate collaboration with colleagues, you could try sharing one or two strategies that you use with English language learners.) List your ideas.

To maximize English language learners' opportunities for success in school, teachers must work together toward a shared mission and vision under strong, supportive leadership. School staff members need to build consensus from well-articulated goals that are formulated and supported by all constituents, including students, parents, and the community at large. Over time, by working together, school personnel can become a cohesive force that unifies, solidifies, sustains, and advocates for language education (Gottlieb & Nguyen, 2007).

Collaboration among teachers serving English language learners helps to

- build trust, respect, and appreciation for educators' respective professional roles

- dispel potential stereotyping and prejudice against language or cultural groups

- shape a common understanding of the second language acquisition process along with the linguistic and cultural assets of second language learners

- agree on students' levels of English language proficiency as related to grade-level academic expectations

- afford students access to a common, standards-based curriculum

- craft appropriate and fair assessment and grading practices

- ensure continuity of language support services for English language learners

The roles of language and content teachers

When language and content teachers work together, they maximize learning opportunities for English language learners. As Figure 5.6 shows, the two groups have distinct yet complementary roles; collaboration results when communication between teachers revolves around a shared set of responsibilities for all students.

Language teachers bring expertise from the areas of linguistics, sociolinguistics, psycholinguistics, cultural diversity, second language acquisition, second language methodologies, and language-related instructional strategies and assessment. With a solid grounding in the language side of student learning, language teachers are equipped to work with ELP standards and apply them to their particular settings. On the other hand, content teachers have a deep understanding of the knowledge and skills associated with specific content areas and grade levels along with content-related methodologies, instructional strategies, and assessment.

Together the language and content team has a more complete repertoire of teaching approaches to draw on and adapt for English language learners. Through joint planning, language becomes the vehicle for learning content while content provides the context for second language acquisition.

Language Teachers	Collaboration	Content Teachers
select ELP standards and strands of sample performance indicators		select state academic content standards and achievement standards
formulate language objectives		formulate content objectives
identify the vocabulary, language functions, grammatical structures, and discourse of social and academic language		identify content knowledge and skills
include supports/strategies for language learning		include accommodations/ supports for content learning
differentiate language activities and tasks		differentiate content activities and tasks
determine standards-based grading of language development		determine standards-based grading of subject-area achievement

Figure 5.6. The Collaborative Roles of Language and Content Teachers.

All stakeholders should be considered potential collaborators in the design and delivery of services for English language learners. For example, if an English language learner has an individualized education program (IEP) due to a diagnosed disability, then a special education teacher might join the team. If some of the students have had limited or interrupted schooling, then a language resource teacher could also assume team membership. If other students have a solid grounding in their native language, then teachers who are bilingual should be consulted.

Cam recognized that the English language learners in her district were a heterogeneous mix in terms of their eligibility for additional services such as Title I reading and math, gifted and talented, and special education. Professional development revolving around the TESOL English language proficiency standards had helped all staff members to understand their importance in guiding the academic language development of all students. Thus, the standards had become a tool to promote collaboration among educators. Seeing the kindergartners smile as the middle school English language learners marched in for the weekly Book Brigade made Cam proud of this collaborative effort between teachers at different schools.

Task 5.2. Forming a Collaborative Team

How might you work with other educators in your school or district to coordinate the language education program of your English language learners? Think about the individual English language learners in your teaching context. Then use the chart below to identify potential collaborators and ways to cooperate.

English Language Learners	Educators to Partner With	Ideas for Collaboration
students with IEPs		
gifted and talented students		
students with limited or interrupted formal schooling		
long-term students receiving multiple support services		
newcomers with strong L1 literacy		
reclassified or transitioned students		

Ideas for structuring collaboration

Collaboration can be enhanced by providing ongoing professional development to teams (e.g., a language teacher, a content teacher, and an administrator) rather than to individual teachers. By creating learning communities, language and content teachers can work side by side for the benefit of all students. Data show that content teachers want to serve all their students, yet they may not have the necessary tools to do so (Gándara, Maxwell-Jolly, & Driscoll, 2005); that's where language teachers can substantively contribute to the discussion.

Collaborative teams can work on designing services for English language learners with a shared mission and goals. Together, team members can

- develop curriculum that is engaging, perhaps thematic or interdisciplinary
- use big ideas generated from the topics list for the ELP standards (see Appendix A)
- differentiate activities by levels of English language proficiency and content knowledge
- decide how to assess students, from both a language and a content perspective
- agree on grading practices, such as the use of rubrics

Collaborative teams can also work to establish common grading criteria that are differentiated according to students' levels of English language proficiency. For example, teams can weigh the relative merits of allowing progress and achievement to factor into grading practices. Thus, to some extent, teams can base grades on the efforts of students at the lower end of the English language proficiency scale, who demonstrate progress over time, and on the achievements of English language learners who have reached a threshold of English language proficiency (Gottlieb, 2006).

Grading practices can be translated into standards-based reporting forms. Language and content teachers can combine efforts in the design of reporting forms such as the one shown in Figure 5.7. In this form, the TESOL English language proficiency standards, in the left-hand column, address the four language domains. Each standard is seen alongside its corresponding academic content area, on the right, so that all teachers working with English language learners understand the relationship between language proficiency and achievement.

Task 5.3. Collaborating on Grading and Reporting

Figure 5.7 is one example of a form for reporting standards-based information on English language learners. How could you adapt it to better represent collaboration between language and content teachers?

Draft a reporting or grading form for your grade, school, or district. As you do so, think about the following:

- How can language proficiency data and academic achievement data be displayed so that parents and students understand the differences between the two sets?

- Who might collaborate to develop the form (e.g., language and content teachers or a committee with administrative representation)?

- How might you jointly decide with other teachers or administrators on grading policies for your English language learners?

There is no formula for teacher collaboration, because the climate of every school and the personalities of every staff are distinctive. Most schools have limited time available for professional development activities. For teachers to cooperate, they need to have a keen sense of their individual contributions to the coordinated effort. The checklist in Figure 5.8 delineates possible roles in the education of English language learners. Teachers, when paired or grouped, should bring complementary areas of expertise so that together they can craft a sound instructional program for their English language learners. Through their strengths, teachers can begin the conversation regarding how to maximize educational opportunities for their students.

	English Language Proficiency Student's English (L2) Language Proficiency Level: ____					**Academic Achievement** Native Language (L1): ____	
	Listening	Speaking	Reading	Writing		In L2	In L1
Language of Language Arts					**Language Arts**		
Language of Math	Listening	Speaking	Reading	Writing	**Math**	In L2	In L1
Language of Science	Listening	Speaking	Reading	Writing	**Science**	In L2	In L1
Language of Social Studies	Listening	Speaking	Reading	Writing	**Social Studies**	In L2	In L1
Social, Intercultural, and Instructional Language	Listening	Speaking	Reading	Writing	**Fine Arts**		
					Physical Education / Health		

Figure 5.7. A Collaborative Reporting Form for English Language Learners. Adapted from Gottlieb (2006, p. 176).

As a teacher working with English language learners, I understand . . .

- ❏ the stages of English language development for second language learners
- ❏ the role of native language in English language development
- ❏ the home cultures of the students
- ❏ the English language demands of the classroom
- ❏ the content demands of the classroom
- ❏ the expectations of English language learners and their English-proficient peers
- ❏ how to scaffold language
- ❏ how to scaffold content
- ❏ how to support language learning through differentiated instruction
- ❏ how to support content learning through differentiated instruction
- ❏ how to work with English language proficiency standards
- ❏ how to work with academic content standards
- ❏ how to interpret language proficiency data
- ❏ how to interpret academic achievement data

Figure 5.8. A Checklist to Guide Teacher Collaboration.

Task 5.4. Teacher Voices in Collaboration

Use the checklist in Figure 5.8 to help create a team devoted to teaching English language learners. First, complete the checklist and identify your contributions to the team. Then seek out colleagues who will balance your strengths. Together, you can maximize your collective expertise in serving English language learners in your school or district.

➤ How can school and district leaders stimulate collaboration?

Many types of educators are responsible for the education of English language learners in their schools and districts. Figure 5.9 lists some of the leaders who work with English language learners in schools and districts.

Examples of School Leaders	Examples of District Leaders
instructional coaches	directors or coordinators of programs, projects, or services
lead or mentoring teachers	specialists and consultants
department heads	assistant superintendents
supervisors or team leaders	superintendents or chief education officers
assistant principals	
principals	

Figure 5.9. Examples of School and District Leaders Involved in the Education of English Language Learners.

Task 5.5. Case Study: An Example of Non-Collaboration

Juan Morales is a Spanish-speaking second grader who has just been brought up for case study for potential learning disabilities. He began his educational career in an English-only preschool, with his native language not fully developed and little English language proficiency. As a kindergartner, he qualified for the district's bilingual education program and began literacy development in Spanish. In first grade, he received Reading First services, which were only available in English to struggling readers.

By second grade, Juan was seen by a pull-out reading resource teacher because his English language literacy had not kept up with that of his peers. At the same time, some native language instruction was maintained by an itinerant teacher a couple of times a week. Juan's underachievement in English and in Spanish prompted his second-grade classroom teacher to investigate the possibility of special education involvement.

Based on this scenario, answer the following questions:

1. Does Juan's current performance in school stem from a language and cultural difference, a learning difficulty, or discontinuity of language support? What evidence might you need to collect to justify your response?

2. How would having a collaborative leadership team that creates district language policies prevent situations like Juan's from occurring?

3. How could district and school leaders encourage teachers to communicate from grade to grade, thereby enhancing Juan's opportunities for academic success? What could have been done to promote articulation in Juan's education from year to year?

The case study described in Task 5.5 exemplifies student failure brought about by systemic deficiencies in the teaching/learning environment, not in the English language learner (Artiles & Ortiz, 2002). Specifically, the inconsistency in services provided and languages of instruction, coupled with the lack of articulation between teachers from year to year, has compromised this young English language learner's language, literacy, and academic development in not one but two languages.

School leaders can prevent situations like Juan's by encouraging collaboration among staff members. Like teachers, school leaders are faced with a myriad of daily challenges. Nevertheless, the school principal must epitomize instructional leadership by consistently communicating the school's mission throughout the building and by setting a climate of high expectations for all students. Following are six ideas for building-level administrators to nurture collaboration among all school personnel.

Six Steps to Creating a Collaborative Environment

1. **Allocate dedicated time for collaboration.**

2. **Create a rich learning environment.**

3. **Advocate on behalf of the students and their family members.**

4. **Ensure continuity of language services from grade to grade.**

5. **Encourage professional development and teacher learning communities.**

6. **Implement strategies that maximize the integration of language and content.**

---

1. Allocate dedicated time for collaboration.

Time is a precious commodity in schools, but it is critical that a dedicated segment be created for teachers working with English language learners. School administrators can stimulate and facilitate teacher collaboration by carving out dedicated time for meetings, professional development, professional learning communities, or even informal grade or cross-grade discussion. For example, by scheduling a monthly brown-bag lunch around a book study for teachers at adjacent grade levels, an elementary principal can create time for teachers to share information.

Administrators have the power to develop policies that give teachers

- joint planning time with other teachers, coaches, or mentors
- time to discuss student progress
- grade-level or team time
- school-wide committee time
- professional development time
- time to coordinate educational services

2. Create a rich learning environment.

Schools should be inviting places that welcome and relish linguistic and cultural diversity. All students need to be exposed to and involved in learning experiences that stem from stimulating learning environments, both inside the classroom and around the school.

The school and the classroom, as microcosms of our pluralistic society, should contain

- evidence of multiculturalism and multilingualism
- evidence of original student work on walls and in corridors
- evidence of the value of literacy and print in multiple languages and media
- evidence of student-centered, hands-on learning

3. Advocate on behalf of the students and their family members.

Research on effective schools has identified the importance of establishing relationships between students' homes and their schools. Strong administrators support students, family members, and the communities in which the schools reside. A coordination of effort among community partners promotes a unified spirit. School leaders should, when feasible, use the languages of the families and neighborhood to attract and maintain communication with parents and others outside the school. If unfamiliar with the students' native languages and cultures, school leaders should involve appropriate teachers, paraprofessionals, and community organizations or agencies in the communication process.

Administrators, as educational advocates, are

- facilitators of a shared mission, vision, goals, and expectations
- supporters of teachers, students, family members, and communities
- believers in the potential of all students and teachers
- policy makers who promote fairness, equity, and access to learning for all students
- consistent implementers who strive for continuous improvement of teaching and learning
- leaders of educational programs

4. Ensure continuity of language services from grade to grade.

A continuous flow of information about students from year to year is vital for teachers. Administrative support and a synchronized instructional design for language education programs are essential starting points for building collaboration from grade to grade and from school to school within a district.

Continuity of language services for English language learners can be provided through

- articulation of standards for instruction and assessment
- a spiraling and scaffolded curriculum that addresses language through content
- frequent monitoring of student progress in language development and academic achievement

- documentation of student performance through a uniform, standards-based grading system

- use of standard or common assessments, designed for English language learners, across grades

- time to discuss individual students and their accomplishments or challenges as they transition from programs or to the next grade

5. Encourage professional development and teacher learning communities.

Sustained professional development offers educators opportunities to gain an understanding of the research and theoretical bases for teaching, acquire new instructional strategies designed for English language learners, and discuss how to apply this knowledge to their schools and classrooms. These new ideas and insights can be reinforced through professional learning communities, in which teachers and administrators may delve into issues and grapple with challenges that affect teaching and learning. The purpose of this devoted time together is to share learning and then act on what has been learned, thereby seeking school improvement through continuous inquiry.

6. Implement strategies that maximize the integration of language and content.

In today's heterogeneous classrooms, traditional teaching methodologies that focus on whole-class instruction do not meet the needs of individual students. School leaders can seek ways to allow teachers with specializations to work side by side with classroom teachers to develop classroom activities that include a variety of instructional strategies to engage students. Many students, including English language learners, can benefit from specific strategies to bolster their academic language.

To enable teachers to maximize the integration of language and content for their English language learners, administrators should

- encourage teachers to participate in coaching or co-teaching practices

- pair veteran teachers with those who have less experience

- provide opportunities for teachers to form study groups or professional learning communities

- allocate space on school and district electronic mailing lists for teachers to discuss and share ideas

- give teachers a voice in reorganizing or restructuring language education programs

- revamp curriculum so that it is aligned with and reflective of both English language proficiency standards and academic content standards

- train all staff in instructional strategies that integrate language and content

The following real-life episode illustrates the value of teachers working together.

Language and Mainstream Teachers Co-Teaching

In the past few years, we, as English as a second language (ESL) teachers in our suburban school district, have felt that the trend for instructing English language learners was moving into the mainstream classroom and co-teaching content-area curriculum. At our request, the central administration of our district supported us by hiring a consultant to lead a 15-hour study group. My co-teacher is a veteran Grade 5 classroom teacher with math as her strongest area of expertise, and I have been an ESL teacher for 14 years.

Last year, as part of our reorganization process for this fall, we took all of the Grade 4 English language learners in our school—who had been distributed in several classes—and placed them together in one Grade 5 classroom. In addition, there are several former English language learners and special education students in the class.

Since ESL teachers have begun collaborating and co-teaching with classroom teachers at a level heretofore not attempted in our school, we have seen other support personnel starting to co-teach as well. Reading specialists and special educators have joined us, not only at our school but across our district, in aligning their instruction more and more with content-area teachers and pushing in to co-teach.

Joseph Gottschalk
ESL Teacher
West Harrison, NY

► How can the TESOL English language proficiency standards foster collaboration among stakeholders?

To evoke systemic change that leads to achieving high and equitable levels of student learning, collaboration has to be strong and enduring. We believe that the TESOL ELP standards can be the impetus for stimulating such educational change.

Strong alliances are forged through collaboration. The following two examples from the field illustrate partnerships between universities and educators that center on implementing standards-based education for English language learners.

A University–School District Partnership

One example of successful school-university partnerships is that of the long-term working relationship between professors from George Mason University and staff from the Fairfax County public schools. This team of educators has worked collaboratively for over 15 years to bring current research and theory into practice on a continual basis. Aspects of collaboration have included developing, refining, and implementing performance-based English language proficiency assessments, as well as providing professional development on their administration and establishing inter-rater reliability in scoring.

The assessment tasks and rubrics have been developed in alignment with state language arts standards as part of district-wide ESOL program placement assessments. The most recent collaborative efforts have focused on refining the assessments based on teacher and university feedback and realigning them with new state English language proficiency and revised language arts standards. The partnership extends to classroom-based assessments that support teaching English through the content areas at the secondary level, and a writing rubric that can be used as part of formative assessment for students in Grades 1-3. With a focus on incorporating current research and theory into daily classroom practice, this team plans on continuing its long-term university-school district partnership into the future.

Lorraine Valdez Pierce
Associate Professor,
George Mason University

Teddi Predaris
Director, ESOL Office,
Fairfax County Public Schools

A University–Teacher Educator Partnership

The TESOL English language proficiency (ELP) standards have been the impetus for the University of Guam's Micronesian Language Institute and the Guam public school system's teachers and administrators (including a school board member) to collaborate within the venue of a credit-bearing course. This initiative was made possible through the Guam ESL Certification Plus project, a U.S. Department of Education Title III professional development grant. Administrative support, leadership, networking, and advocacy from the sponsoring institution have prompted ongoing collaboration that has been instrumental to the success of the project.

The kick-off was a 4-day workshop for which graduate or undergraduate course credit was offered; participants reviewed and reached consensus on the ELP standards and the individual features of the standards matrix. During this initial phase, teachers from across the island then divided into grade-level clusters, agreed to have cluster meetings at rotating schools, and planned to reunite as a whole group on vacation days (even the day after Thanksgiving!) or Saturdays. In between face-to-face meetings, team members communicated through e-mail. To illustrate the commitment of the group, an instructional coach and an administrator volunteered to review the multiple drafts and provide guidance.

In phase 2 of the course (between drafts 4 and 5 of the ELP standards), the instructor facilitated discussion and review. Grade-level clusters analyzed each other's work and provided feedback. In addition, there was opportunity for reflection on the process; in response to the question "What accomplishment are you proudest of so far?" the number one response was collaboration with grade-level-cluster teammates.

By being integral to the development process, team members realized the value of collaboration and how it led to ownership and pride in the product. Consequently, the Guam English language proficiency standards will ultimately bear a TESOL imprint with a distinctive island signature.

> Rosa Salas Palomo
> Director, University of Guam Micronesian Language Institute
>
> Margo Gottlieb
> Teacher Educator and Course Instructor

"English language learners struggle to balance language and content, while educators need partnerships and specific professional learning" (Nordmeyer, 2008, p. 34). We, as language educators, owe it to our profession and our students to forge alliances with other teachers and staff members and to seek the support of our administrators and the communities that we serve.

Reflect and Respond

In this chapter, we illustrate how collaboration among teachers, school leaders, and other stakeholders facilitates English language learners' access to grade-level curriculum while taking their English language proficiency levels into account. Drawing on these discussions, consider the following questions:

- What are some short-term steps you could take to promote collaboration in your setting?

- What long-range planning would be needed to establish more systemic changes?

- Who could be involved in your collaborative efforts?

Vignette Revisited

The humanities team had learned valuable lessons through implementing the English language proficiency standards as part of a collaborative venture with the neighboring kindergarten teachers. The middle school students were enthusiastic and responsive to helping their young buddies and pleased to be simultaneously meeting their own grade-level language objectives.

The humanities team and kindergarten teachers remained in communication through group e-mail, documenting and sharing the progress for both groups of students through narratives. The teachers decided that it was important for the students themselves to provide part of the feedback for this new venture. Each pair of buddies maintained a journal of books read, thereby engaging in self-assessment and reflection on their literacy development.

The entire school district was promoting collaboration through team-building and was using the TESOL English language proficiency standards as the vehicle to coalesce teacher groups. By working together and developing common goals for their students' English language development and academic achievement, the teachers gained new respect for their students, their colleagues, and their profession.

Chapter 6
Personalizing the Use of the TESOL English Language Proficiency Standards Through Transformations

The real process of education should be the process of learning to think through the application of real problems.

—John Dewey

Guiding Questions

➤ **How can strands of sample performance indicators be adapted to meet the needs of individual classrooms?**

➤ **What are some types and examples of transformations?**

➤ **How can teachers determine the need for new strands of sample performance indicators?**

➤ **How can new strands of sample performance indicators be created for individual classrooms?**

Vignette

Daniela Armida taught an eighth-grade bilingual math class. When she first learned about the TESOL English language proficiency standards, Daniela realized that they could help her identify the language needs of the students in her class. However, the sample topics listed in the matrix for Standard 3, the language of math, weren't applicable to her upcoming unit on line segments and angles. How could Daniela use the sample performance indicators as a starting point for planning her lesson? How could she expand their usefulness for her classroom and her students?

Although the English language proficiency standards are fixed, their components, such as the sample performance indicators (SPIs), are flexible and are designed so that teachers can adapt them to meet the instructional and assessment needs of individual classrooms. Being able to personalize strands of sample performance indicators means that educators can align the ELP standards to a district's curriculum or match them with teachers' individual instruction and assessment practices. This chapter explores how SPIs can be adapted or transformed to support language learning in a range of classrooms.

➤ How can strands of sample performance indicators be adapted to meet the needs of individual classrooms?

As described in chapter 3, each SPI consists of three elements: language function, topic, and support. By changing or *transforming* one or more of these elements, teachers can customize their use of the English language proficiency standards in the classroom. *Transformations* are changes in the strands of SPIs to meet the needs of students in a specific instructional context. Such transformations provide teachers and administrators with almost endless possibilities for adapting the English language proficiency standards.

Transformations are necessary because the strands of SPIs in the standards matrices are only a small, representative sample of the many ways in which the ELP standards can be implemented. As previously explained, the strands were based on numerous source documents including state academic content standards for language arts, mathematics, science, and social studies and content standards from several national organizations. If all these standards were to have a presence in the TESOL ELP standards, the result would be an unmanageable compendium.

Teachers may choose to make transformations to the language function, the topic, or the support of a strand of SPIs. Changes may be necessary for a variety of reasons: for example, to reflect the availability of resources (such as support materials), to maintain students' motivation in a learning task, to offer students multiple ways to access content through language, or to reinforce students' language learning. Additional reasons for each type of transformation follow.

Possible reasons for changes in *language function* are

- to expand the language repertoire of a group of students at a designated level of English language proficiency

- to reinforce language introduced at a designated level of English language proficiency

- to offer a variety of possible language structures for a lesson

- to represent authentic language use in the classroom

- to make connections between language domains

- to design integrated activities, with a focus such as oral language (listening and speaking), literacy (reading and writing), or comprehension (listening and reading)

Possible reasons for changes in *topic* are

- to match the language strands to the content of a lesson or unit of study

- to differentiate language instruction for English language learners irrespective of content topics

- to facilitate collaboration between language and content teachers through the use of common topics
- to ensure alignment with academic content standards
- to match district or school curriculum
- to reflect a particular thematic unit of study
- to coordinate units of study with grade-level teams

Possible reasons for changes in *support* are

- to increase opportunities for students at the earliest levels of English language proficiency to access content through language
- to offer varied support at each level of English language proficiency
- to match types of support with available teacher resources and students' learning styles
- to enhance the meaning of a particular communication for English language learners

We believe that, through transformations, all educators working with English language learners can have input into the development and implementation of standards-based curriculum, assessment, and instruction. By engaging in transformations, educators can apply the English language proficiency standards to their particular settings and students. Teachers and administrators can

- adapt the elements of SPIs to meet the instructional and assessment needs of individual classrooms and groups of students
- design common formative assessments for language education programs
- develop district-wide curricula for language education programs
- align the strands of SPIs to specific educational philosophies and practices

➤ What are some types and examples of transformations?

Each element of a strand of SPIs—language function, topic, and support—may be transformed in a variety of ways. Transformations may involve substituting, adding, or combining elements.

When one or more elements of an SPI are transformed, the purpose, context, or delivery of a communication shifts—thus more closely fitting a real classroom context. In this way, transformations provide teachers with the flexibility to incorporate the language needs of their students into the framework of the English language proficiency standards.

The next section provides detailed examples of the three different categories of transformations.

Substitution transformations

In a substitution, any of the three elements of an SPI may be exchanged for another example of the same element. Figure 6.1 is a list of types of substitutions. Note that when elements of an SPI are transformed, other changes may also be necessary—for example, in the language domain or in the standard that is being addressed.

Figures 6.2, 6.3, and 6.4 provide examples of how substitution works across the language functions, topics, and supports of individual SPIs or strands of SPIs.

Notice that when the topic is changed (Figure 6.3), an entire strand of SPIs must be transformed.

Substitution transformations include replacing . . .

- one *language function* with another *language function* within the same language domain, level of language proficiency, and standard

- one *language function* with another *language function* to represent a different language domain within a standard

- one *topic* with another *topic* within the same language domain and standard

- one *topic* with another *topic* within the same language domain, but representing a different standard

- one *topic* with another *topic* to represent a different language domain and a different standard

- *topics* across language domains

- one form of *support* with another example of the same form of *support*

- one form of *support* (visual, graphic, or interactive) with another form of *support*

Figure 6.1. Examples of Substitution Transformations.

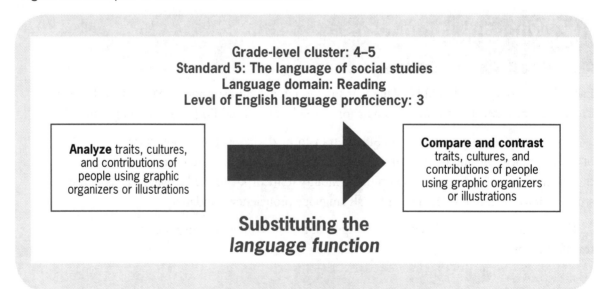

Figure 6.2. Substitution of One Language Function for Another Language Function. Adapted from *PreK–12 English Language Proficiency Standards* (TESOL, 2006, p. 77).

Grade-level cluster: 9–12
Standard 4: The language of science
Language domain: Listening
Levels of English language proficiency: 1–5

Topic	Level 1	Level 2	Level 3	Level 4	Level 5
Nuclear structures and functions	Distinguish parts of elements (e.g., atoms, molecules) from oral statements using visuals, models, or manipulatives	Compare the arrangement of elements (e.g., atoms, ionic crystals, polymers) from oral statements using visual or graphic support	Draw or build models of elements from oral descriptions in small groups	Create representations of the properties, features, and uses of elements from oral descriptions in small groups	Evaluate delivery of oral reports about elements presented by peers

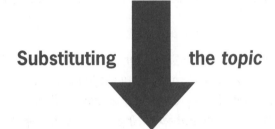

Substituting   the *topic*

Topic	Level 1	Level 2	Level 3	Level 4	Level 5
Food chains	Distinguish phases of **food chains** from oral statements using visuals, models, or manipulatives	Compare phases of **food chains** from oral statements using visual or graphic support	Draw or build models of **food chains** from oral descriptions in small groups	Create representations of phases of **food chains** from oral descriptions in small groups	Evaluate delivery of oral reports about **food chains** presented by peers

Figure 6.3. Substitution of One Topic for Another Topic. Adapted from *PreK–12 English Language Proficiency Standards* (TESOL, 2006, p. 94).

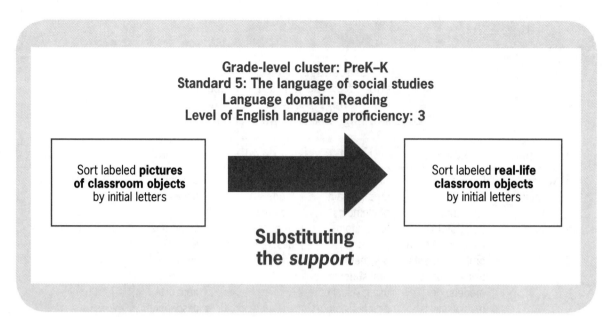

Figure 6.4. Substitution of One Form of Support for Another Example of the Same Form of Support. Adapted from *PreK–12 English Language Proficiency Standards* (TESOL, 2006, p. 57).

As she planned her unit on line segments and angles, Daniela looked through the strands of SPIs for topics that might lend themselves to transformation. She saw a strand on the topic of Volume and realized that she could create a new strand fairly easily by substituting a different topic. Figure 6.5 shows the strand of SPIs Daniela started with.

Standard 3: The language of mathematics
Grade-level cluster: 6–8
Language domain: Speaking

Topic	Level 1	Level 2	Level 3	Level 4	Level 5
Volume	Name figures or dimensions from real objects or diagrams	Define dimensions of figures based on objects or diagrams using general language (e.g., "Height goes up and down.")	Describe dimensions of objects or diagrams using some specialized language (e.g., "You times base by height.")	Analyze figures or operations in real-life situations using specialized language (e.g., "You multiply base by height of walls to know how much paint you need.")	Explain differences in usage among operations and figures using specialized or technical language

Figure 6.5. A Strand of Sample Performance Indicators From ELP Standard 3 (Topic: Volume). Adapted from *PreK–12 English Language Proficiency Standards* (TESOL, 2006, p. 82).

When Daniela was finished, her new strand of SPIs offered a solid basis for differentiating instruction for her English language learners as they started this complex unit. Figure 6.6 shows the result of her transformations.

Standard 3: The language of mathematics
Grade-level cluster: 6–8
Language domain: Speaking

Topic	Level 1	Level 2	Level 3	Level 4	Level 5
Line segments and angles	Name line segments and angles from real objects or diagrams	Define dimensions of line segments and angles based on objects or diagrams using general language (e.g., "Segment AB is longer than segment CD.")	Describe dimensions of line segments and angles using some specialized language (e.g., "Line A is parallel to line B.")	Analyze line segments and angles in real-life situations using specialized language (e.g., "On the map, find a street that is perpendicular to another street.")	Explain differences in usage among line segments and angles using specialized or technical language

Figure 6.6. SPI Created for Geometry Unit Through Transformation. Adapted from *PreK–12 English Language Proficiency Standards* (TESOL, 2006, p. 82).

Task 6.1. Transforming One Element of an SPI

Transform this sample performance indicator by substituting *one* element: the language function, the topic, or the form of support. Think about how the SPI might be customized to fit your English language learners.

Grade-level cluster: 1–3
Standard 5: The language of social studies
Language domain: Reading
Topic: Time and chronology
Level of English language proficiency: 2

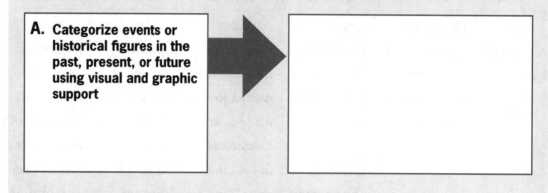

A. Categorize events or historical figures in the past, present, or future using visual and graphic support

Now transform the other elements through substitution.

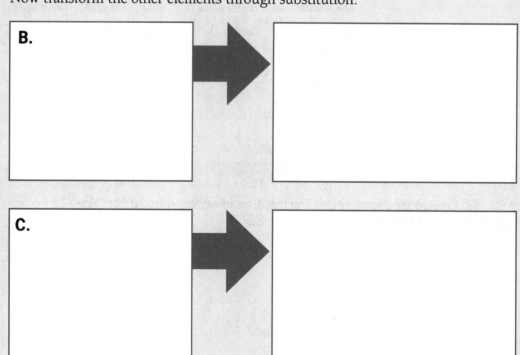

B.

C.

A template for practicing more transformations can be found in Appendix D.

Addition transformations

Adding elements to sample performance indicators can increase their clarity and focus. By adding specific supports, topics, or language functions to SPIs, teachers can ensure that the strands are useful for planning their own instruction and assessment. Figure 6.7 lists some types of addition transformations.

The transformation in Figure 6.8 illustrates how to enhance strands of SPIs through addition. In bilingual classrooms, like Daniela's, the use of the native language (L1) for support is a valuable option.

Addition transformations include adding . . .

- a second *language function*
- a second *support* of the same form (visual, graphic, or interactive)
- a second *support* of a different form
- examples of specific *supports*
- examples of *subtopics*
- examples of *language structures*

Figure 6.7. Examples of Addition Transformations.

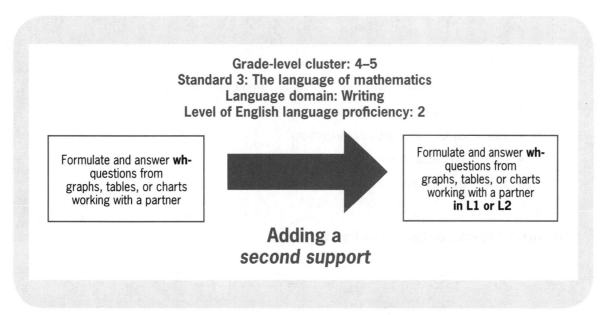

Grade-level cluster: 4–5
Standard 3: The language of mathematics
Language domain: Writing
Level of English language proficiency: 2

Formulate and answer **wh-**questions from graphs, tables, or charts working with a partner

Formulate and answer **wh-**questions from graphs, tables, or charts working with a partner **in L1 or L2**

Adding a
second support

Figure 6.8. Addition of a Second Support of the Same Form (Visual, Graphic, or Interactive). Adapted from *PreK–12 English Language Proficiency Standards* (TESOL, 2006, p. 73).

Task 6.2. Ideas for Addition Transformations

Think about the range of English language proficiency of the English language learners in your class. Then consider the pace at which these students complete classroom tasks. How could the use of addition transformations help you differentiate your teaching to better meet your students' individual needs? Jot down a couple of ideas.

Combination transformations

Combination transformations involve the use of two or more types of transformations within or across strands of SPIs. To design standards-based oral language or literacy activities for English language learners, for example, teachers may *add* language domains and *substitute* topics; in doing so, they create *combination* transformations. Units of instruction and projects also lend themselves to a mixture of transformation types. Combination transformations may be created by reconfiguring any SPI elements, as shown in Figure 6.9. Although they are a bit more complex than the other categories, mixed transformations yield untold numbers of ways to match SPIs and the English language proficiency standards with real-life teaching situations.

Figure 6.10 shows how two SPIs may be joined at a given level of English language proficiency. In this example, the topic of *Colors* from the listening SPI is dropped and the topic of *Community helpers* from the speaking SPI is retained. This transformation demonstrates both the close connection between listening and speaking in the classroom and the role of oral language acquisition in developing academic language proficiency.

Combination transformations include combining . . .

- substitution and addition transformations
- substitution and combination transformations
- addition and combination transformations
- substitution, addition, and combination transformations

Figure 6.9. Examples of Combination Transformations.

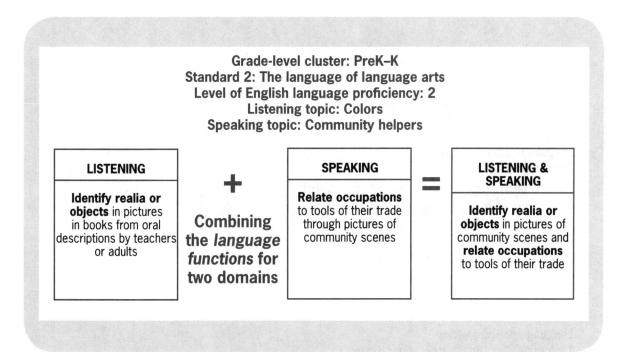

Grade-level cluster: PreK–K
Standard 2: The language of language arts
Level of English language proficiency: 2
Listening topic: Colors
Speaking topic: Community helpers

LISTENING		SPEAKING		LISTENING & SPEAKING
Identify realia or objects in pictures in books from oral descriptions by teachers or adults	**+** Combining the *language functions* for two domains	**Relate occupations** to tools of their trade through pictures of community scenes	**=**	**Identify realia or objects** in pictures of community scenes and **relate occupations** to tools of their trade

Figure 6.10. A Combination of Language Functions for Listening and Speaking (Oral Language) Within the Same Language Proficiency Level. Adapted from *PreK–12 English Language Proficiency Standards* (TESOL, 2006, p. 50).

Figures 6.11 and 6.12 illustrate how several transformations can take place. First, read the individual SPIs in Figure 6.11. Then consider how they are combined in Figure 6.12. Through multiple transformations, the domains are *combined*, a new topic is *substituted*, and additional elements are *added*. The following questions guided this process of combining elements:

1. Which language domains are to be added together within a grade-level cluster, and for what purpose?

2. What topic or subtopic is to be substituted, and does it reflect the same standard or another standard?

3. Which levels of language proficiency are to be affected by the transformations?

4. What additional supports might be useful for English language learners?

As a tool that is teacher driven and shaped, the transformation of sample performance indicators has tremendous potential use in the classroom. Language teachers can decide which elements of SPIs are most beneficial for their students, or they can work in conjunction with content teachers to plan the delivery of instruction and assessment. By allowing teachers to manipulate the elements within the strands of SPIs, the English language proficiency standards become personal, relevant, and useful.

Grade-level cluster: 6–8
Standard 4: The language of science
Language domains: Reading, Writing
Levels of English language proficiency: 2 and 3

Language domain: Reading
Topics: Body systems, Organs

Level 2	Level 3
Classify short descriptions of systems (e.g., respiratory or digestive) using visual or graphic support	Find or sort visually or graphically supported information about processes (e.g., veins vs. arteries)

Language domain: Writing
Topics: Weather, Climate zones, Natural disasters

Level 2	Level 3
Describe features, conditions, or occurrences around the world based on newspapers, the Internet, or illustrated text	Compare features, conditions, or occurrences between two areas (e.g., native country and the United States) using information from multiple sources

Figure 6.11. Sample Performance Indicators From ELP Standard 4 (Domains: Reading and Writing). Adapted from *PreK–12 English Language Proficiency Standards* (TESOL, 2006, p. 85).

Combined language domains: Reading and writing
Substituted topic: Forms of energy
Added subtopics: Light, sound, heat
Added support: Graphic organizers

> Combining *language domains*, substituting the *topic*, and adding *subtopics* and *support*

Level 2	Level 3
Classify short descriptions of forms of energy (e.g., light, sound, heat) using visual or graphic support and describe their features using graphic organizers	Find visually or graphically supported information about forms of energy (e.g., light, sound, heat) from multiple sources and compare their features using graphic organizers

Figure 6.12. SPIs Created Through a Combination of Substitution, Addition, and Combination Transformations.

Task 6.3. Using Multiple Transformations

Select two or more types of transformations (substitution, addition, or combination) that might be useful in your teaching situation. Then choose an SPI or a strand of SPIs for your grade-level cluster. Refer to *PreK–12 English Language Proficiency Standards* (TESOL, 2006) or to the example SPIs reprinted in this volume.

Use multiple transformations to create new SPIs to match your classroom context. Write out your transformations using the form in Appendix D. As you work, ask yourself these four questions:

1. Which language domains are to be added together within a grade-level cluster, and for what purpose?

2. What topic or subtopic is to be substituted, and does it reflect the same standard or another standard?

3. Which levels of language proficiency are to be affected by the transformations?

4. What additional supports might be useful for English language learners?

What value do you see in being able to create mixed transformations to use in your standards-based classroom?

➤ How can teachers determine the need for new strands of sample performance indicators?

In designing effective language education programs for English language learners, teachers may find that transformations alone will not address underlying issues and needs within their teaching context. One of the major issues language educators face is the degree of alignment between the TESOL English language proficiency standards and the standards established by a state or other entity. When a disparity exists, teachers may need to design new strands of SPIs. By analyzing the features of the TESOL ELP standards matrix and the elements of its sample performance indicators, teachers can determine whether or not they need to create new strands of SPIs.

To facilitate that decision, a checklist for comparing the TESOL English language proficiency standards with those of your state or other entity is presented in Figure 6.13. If your answer to most of the questions is *no*, then there is a mismatch between the two sets of standards. If that is the case, it would be best to design entirely new sample performance indicators that align with the requirements in your setting.

Given the TESOL English language proficiency standards . . .	YES	NO
1. Do the grade-level clusters correspond to those of your state or entity?		
2. Are the performance definitions for the levels of English language proficiency comparable to those of your state or entity?		
3. Do the topics match those of your school or district curriculum?		
4. Is some type of support—visual, graphic, or interactive—built into the performance indicators for your state's English language proficiency standards?		
5. Are the strands of SPIs compatible with the materials you are using?		

Figure 6.13. A Checklist for Determining the Need for Additional Strands of Sample Performance Indicators.

➤ How can new strands of sample performance indicators be created for individual classrooms?

Designing new strands of SPIs may be the best solution for ensuring a good fit between English language proficiency standards and the academic demands of individual classrooms. In this case, then, the TESOL ELP standards become a model for the design process.

Step 1: Choose a standard, a topic, and a language domain.

The first step in creating a new strand of sample performance indicators is to decide which ELP standard, topic, and language domain(s) the SPIs will reflect. When choosing a topic, teachers should take into consideration how closely the topic fits the requirements of their school or district curriculum and how well it aligns with required standards. In most cases, topic choices reflect grade-level curricula. The new strand of SPIs may focus on one or more language domains. Each decision made in this step should reflect the instructional needs of the designer's teaching context and students. Thus, it will serve as a foundation for the new strand.

Task 6.4. Laying the Foundation for a New Strand of SPIs

Imagine that you are going to design a strand of SPIs to meet the needs of your English language learners and your teaching context. Begin by following the directions in Step 1. Record your decisions here:

Standard: _____   Topic: _____

Grade Level: _____   Language Domain(s): _____

Step 2: Learn the levels of English language proficiency.

It is critical for educators to develop a sense of the levels of English language proficiency. The performance definitions in Figure 3.1 can help to guide understanding of the criteria that underlie the strands of SPIs. To see how these definitions work at targeted grade levels, teachers may find it useful to mix up the cells in a strand of SPIs from the ELP standards matrix, sort them out by levels of English language proficiency, and then analyze the developmental progression across the five levels. Task 6.5 provides an example of such an activity.

Task 6.5. Identifying the Levels of English Language Proficiency

Grade-level cluster: 6–8
Standard 4: The language of science
Language domain: Listening
Topics: Atoms, Cells, Molecules

The SPIs in this strand (from TESOL, 2006, p. 84) are reprinted below in random order. Read the SPIs and then number them according to their language proficiency levels, from Level 1 (Starting) to Level 5 (Bridging). You may wish to consult the performance definitions in Figure 3.1. Then check your responses below.

	Arrange models or diagrams based on sequential oral directions (e.g., stages of mitosis or fission)
	Design or construct models or diagrams from decontextualized oral discourse
	Identify elements within models or diagrams according to oral directions
	Reproduce models or diagrams based on visually supported tapes, CDs, videos, or lectures
	Match oral descriptions of functions of various elements with models or diagrams

(3, 5, 1, 4, 2)

Step 3: Build the strand one SPI at a time, beginning at Level 5.

A strand of sample performance indicators must be built one SPI at a time. Three elements need to be included in every SPI. These elements follow a consistent sequence: (a) language function, (b) topic, and (c) support. The choice of language function emerges from an understanding of topic and grade-level content standards and instructional objectives. It also is related to level of language proficiency.

To begin developing a strand of SPIs, teachers should start with the SPI for the highest level of language proficiency (i.e., Level 5) and work backwards to Level 1. Level 5 is the developmental target of language proficiency instruction and is the level most closely connected to academic content standards. Thus, it serves as a guidepost for the development of SPIs at the remaining proficiency levels.

When writing individual SPIs, it may be helpful to review the discussion of each SPI element found in chapter 4; the material there will provide ideas for this step in the design process. Figure 6.14 illustrates the flow in creating strands of SPIs. A template for developing strands of sample performance indicators is provided in Appendix E.

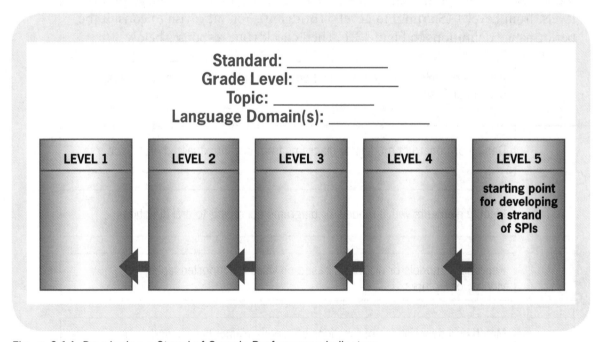

Figure 6.14. Developing a Strand of Sample Performance Indicators.

Step 4: Evaluate the new strand of SPIs.

The checklist in Figure 6.15 provides the criteria used to develop the strands of sample performance indicators in the TESOL ELP standards matrices. These criteria are useful in examining and evaluating new strands of SPIs. The checklist may also be used as a reference in aligning curriculum or designing standards-based lessons or units of study.

	YES	NO
1. Performance definitions for the standards are used as a model to create a developmental progression across the levels of language proficiency.		
2. The expectations for listening, speaking, reading, and writing are adjusted at each grade-level cluster according to the students' ages.		
3. Visual, graphic, or interactive supports are present through Language Proficiency Level 4.		
4. Examples (e.g., language patterns associated with the language function within the context of the standard) are given for clarification or illustration, as warranted.		
5. Linguistic complexity increases with each progressive level of language proficiency.		
6. Specialization of vocabulary increases with each progressive level of language proficiency.		
7. The language function is the first element in each sample performance indicator.		
8. The elements of the sample performance indicators are presented in identical order across the levels of language proficiency.		
9. Listening SPIs are based on oral input, and Reading SPIs are based on written input.		
10. There is consistency in expression and tense across levels of language proficiency (e.g., terms such as *pictures* and *diagrams* or *visual support* and *supported visually* are not interchanged within a strand).		
11. The example topic has been selected from the grade-level cluster list or a subtopic has been substituted.		

Figure 6.15. A Checklist for Designing Strands of Sample Performance Indicators. Adapted from Gottlieb, Cranley, & Oliver (2007, p. RG-39).

Reflect and Respond

This chapter highlights the flexibility of the elements in the TESOL ELP standards matrix by introducing the notion of transformations. Through transformations, teachers can manipulate the elements of SPIs to design standards-based language lessons and units for English language learners that are synchronized with grade-level content and students' language proficiency levels.

Think about how you might guide your instructional and assessment practices by transforming the strands of SPIs. Which types of transformations do you think you will rely on the most, and why? How might you incorporate their use into lesson or unit planning?

Vignette Revisited

Daniela realized that she was not restricted to using the strands of sample performance indicators for Standard 3 (the language of mathematics) from the 6–8 grade-level cluster in teaching geometry to her English language learners. Daniela recognized that the TESOL ELP standards provided a starting place for creating strands of SPIs for use in her lessons and units, and she understood how to adapt and expand them to match the mathematics department's curriculum. Daniela felt that transformations afforded her the additional benefit of being able to incorporate the ELP standards in her classroom every day. In this way, she could be assured that the language of mathematics was integrated into the geometry content.

Chapter 7
Connecting the English Language Proficiency Standards to Curriculum and Instruction

Two roads diverged in a wood, and I—
I took the one less traveled by,
And that has made all the difference.
—Robert Frost

Guiding Questions

➤ **How can teachers incorporate language development into existing approaches for curriculum design?**

➤ **What steps can teachers take to integrate the English language proficiency standards into instructional planning?**

Vignette

Michael Grant loved teaching social studies to middle school students. Michael had been teaching for 20 years; in that time he had noticed the student make-up of the school shift to a mix of students that included English language learners. To design his lessons, he used the district's social studies curriculum, which was based on the state's history and social science standards. Recently Michael had begun working closely with Rachel Numan, the ESL teacher. They had attended a workshop on the TESOL English language proficiency standards together, and they wanted to incorporate these standards into the social studies curriculum to ensure that students learned the necessary language to understand the academic content and to participate actively in lessons.

In this chapter, we present a model for curriculum development that shows how the TESOL English language proficiency (ELP) standards can be used in planning instruction for English language learners at all levels of language proficiency. This model provides the basis for chapters 8 and 9, in which we connect the ELP standards to instructional approaches at the elementary and secondary levels. Our intent in these three chapters is to generate thinking about how to create language-rich instructional environments for English language learners based on the TESOL ELP standards.

➤ How can teachers incorporate language development into existing approaches for curriculum design?

Up to this point, we have emphasized ways in which individual educators can use the ELP standards to meet the academic language needs of their students. However, it is important to acknowledge that teachers operate not only in their classrooms but within a broader context of schools and districts; this means that decisions about instruction are often embedded within established and mandated curricula.

What exactly is a curriculum? For many teachers, a curriculum is a set of printed materials, often a set of binders describing targeted instructional outcomes with suggested paths to achieving those outcomes. In a fourth-grade classroom, for example, the teacher's bookshelf may hold binders that outline the course content for fourth-grade math, language arts, science, and social studies. Given the reform focus of many schools today, the material in these binders may reflect the impact of instructional design frameworks such as *Understanding by Design* (Wiggins & McTighe, 1998) or *Classroom Instruction That Works* (Marzano, Pickering, & Pollock, 2001). Faced with a shelf of binders that embody a set approach to planning content, teachers may puzzle over how to incorporate additional learning targets, such as those illustrated in the ELP standards, into lessons already overflowing with academic content requirements yet containing little focus on language development.

Providing an alternate perspective, Graves (2006) describes curriculum as a dynamic system reflecting a set of processes—planning, enacting, and evaluating—embedded within a specific setting that is influenced by factors such as teacher beliefs, school and district policies, and community expectations. According to this perspective, individual teachers can play an active role in determining both the content of instruction and how that content is taught in individual classrooms.

When teachers decide to weave language instruction into content lessons, they are engaging in a process of changing the curriculum to meet students' needs. To facilitate this process, Gibbons (2006) outlines a multistep framework for integrating language and content: "(1) finding out about learners' language needs, (2) unpacking the mainstream topic for language, (3) selecting the focus language on the basis of this information, (4) designing activities to teach the focus language, and (5) evaluating the unit" (p. 221).

For the first step, teachers investigate learners' existing levels of language knowledge and use: What can students do with language in the classroom as they engage in lesson activities? Teachers gather this information through classroom assessments, including formal assessments and observations.

After gathering information about their learners' language needs, teachers explore the language demands inherent in a unit of instruction. For example, when planning a unit on the reproduction cycle of plants, teachers examine the language that learners will need to participate in the tasks and activities of that unit. This "language inventory" (Gibbons, 2006, p. 225) includes grammatical structures, genres, and vocabulary as well as language domains.

Once both student language needs and the language demands of the content topic have been identified, teachers decide what the focus for language instruction should be. For example, will an instructional activity require students to gather information from reading or to present an argument during a debate? Given students' needs, what language lessons will teachers incorporate into the activity?

Next, teachers design activities that will help students develop the language skills identified in the previous step.

Finally, teachers review the effectiveness of the instructional unit, collecting evidence to determine whether students have learned what was intended and have met the requirements of the curriculum. Teachers also examine whether the instructional activities and tasks were relevant and effective for students at each level of English language proficiency. Information from this step may lead to a revision of the unit.

Task 7.1. Reviewing the Content Curriculum for English Language Learners

The purpose of this task is to raise awareness of the roles of language and content in your curriculum for English language learners. Focus on one grade level or content area if you teach more than one. Consider the following questions in light of Gibbons's framework for integrating language and content. Note your answers in the chart.

Questions	Comments
What is the basis for the organization of your curriculum? What source materials (e.g., standards, textbooks, curriculum frameworks) provide the structure for what you teach?	
To what extent does your curriculum reflect learners' language needs?	
Are language objectives included in the design of units of instruction?	
Do your instructional activities include a focus on language?	
How do you know that your curriculum meets your students' language needs?	

> ➤ **What steps can teachers take to integrate the English language proficiency standards into instructional planning?**

In the previous section, we examined the recursive nature of curriculum design and considered, through Gibbons's framework, how instructional units can integrate both language and content. In this section, we focus on incorporating language into the content curriculum and show how the ELP standards can be used as a resource to modify an existing curriculum or develop a new one. Starting from Gibbons's model, we have created a standards-based framework for this curriculum development process consisting of three phases: previewing, planning, and reflecting. This multistep language curriculum framework can be found in Figure 7.1, followed by explanations and examples.

Previewing: What is the context for language instruction?

Effective instruction emerges from an understanding of student strengths and needs and an analysis of the challenges students may face as they encounter the learning aims set for specific content areas at their grade level. Like the first steps of Gibbons's curriculum design process, the previewing phase requires teachers to reflect on two facets of the teaching context in order to gather information that will inform instructional planning.

Step 1: Determine English language learners' current language profiles.

A critical piece of the needs analysis is determining the proficiency levels of students in the class. If English language proficiency data from the state language test are available, review how the students performed in each language domain to ascertain the range of proficiency levels in the class. Individual student profiles of their performance in each language domain may also be helpful.

A home language survey, given upon entry into a school and completed by a student's parent or guardian, coupled with oral language and literacy surveys completed by students can provide useful information about students' backgrounds and language heritage (Gottlieb, 2006). Examples of such surveys are found in Appendixes F and G.

Teachers can also use the results of various assessments to match student performance in specific content areas (e.g., math or social studies) with one of the five proficiency levels in the ELP standards. Knowing where students are on the proficiency continuum will provide students, teachers, and other stakeholders with a reference point for targeting growth, providing appropriate scaffolding for learning, and measuring achievement.

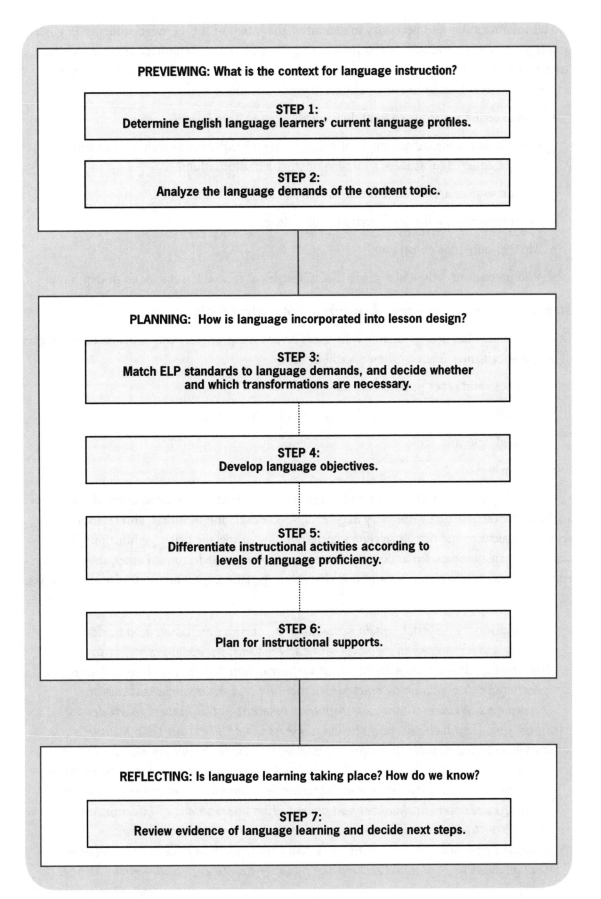

Figure 7.1. A Standards-Based Language Curriculum Framework.

This information is also necessary to determine the extent of "fit" between students' English language proficiency and the context for learning. To get a sense of students' language needs, teachers can gather information about a number of features that will affect how they structure students' learning. Here are some questions to guide this process:

- What specific academic content do students need to learn?

- How flexible is the curriculum? For example, are there district or content standards that must be adhered to? Is there a required textbook or curriculum?

- What resources are available, in L1 as well as L2?

- What options exist for collaboration with colleagues?

- Are there any time constraints?

- Will instruction consist of a single lesson, a series of related lessons, or an in-depth unit?

Step 2: Analyze the language demands of the content topic.

Once the content has been chosen, teachers can review the proposed unit of instruction in terms of language demands. Such a review should include

- textbooks and other printed materials

- additional resources such as multimedia packs or Internet sites

- planned tasks and activities

- assessments

Earlier chapters in this volume provide suggestions for determining these demands, such as a scheme for categorizing vocabulary as general, specialized, and technical, and examples of sentence structures and discourse genres corresponding to specific language functions. These discussions are not intended as complete inventories of language features. Rather, they serve as entry points for teachers into ways of thinking about the language dimensions of academic tasks.

The district's seventh-grade social studies curriculum focused on world history and geography in medieval and early modern times. In preparing to use the ELP standards with the existing curriculum, Michael and Rachel were carefully looking at a unit about Mesoamerican and Andean civilizations to determine the kinds of language demands inherent in the materials students would use. They also reviewed the language needs of all students in Michael's middle school class. Rachel made several suggestions, beginning with an examination of the language proficiency levels of the English language learners in the class to determine where each student fell along the continuum of academic language development. Michael had collected an assortment of information about his students' English language proficiency. From the state English language development scores, he knew that his class had students at all levels, though most were grouped around the middle—Levels 2, 3, and 4 in the TESOL

ELP standards. He also had samples of student performance collected from a range of classroom projects and activities, so he had a fairly clear idea of his students' strengths and of the challenges they faced in specific language domains. He knew, for example, that most of his English language learners needed extra support for their writing assignments.

Task 7.2. Identifying Proficiency Levels

Determine how you can identify the language proficiency levels of English language learners in your class. What types of student data are currently available to you? List them in the chart below next to the appropriate sources.

After you fill in the chart, consider what the available data will tell you about your students' overall language proficiency. For example, will it provide information about your students' skill levels in specific domains (listening, speaking, reading, writing)? What additional information might be helpful in identifying your students' ELP levels, and how could you collect it?

Identifying English Language Proficiency Levels	
Sources	**Types of Information or Data**
Formal classroom assessments	
Informal classroom assessments	
School tests	
District tests	
Other	

Planning: How is language incorporated into lesson design?

In this phase of the model, we focus on a series of steps that teachers can follow to make language an integral part of content lessons for English language learners. At the same time, we note that planning and delivery of lessons can be tackled in many ways. For example, if teachers feel constrained because they lack common planning time, optimal choices may not always be feasible. Also, although we present the steps in a set order, the process itself may not always be linear; within different teaching contexts, some steps may connect more logically in a different sequence than in the order we present them. Nevertheless, the pathway elaborated here highlights important elements that can ensure lessons include a language focus to support student learning across content areas and according to language proficiency levels.

Step 3: Match ELP standards to language demands, and decide whether and which transformations are necessary.

With context information collected and instructional language needs identified, teachers can use the ELP standards as a starting point to identify a range of language targets within content tasks. Note that the broad term *language targets* refers to an assortment of possible language features that may become language objectives in a specific lesson or unit. Teachers should choose targets that correspond to the English language proficiency levels of the students in their classes.

Because the ELP standards are linked to specific content areas, teachers can pinpoint standards to serve as models for planning instruction and assessment by focusing on a strand of sample performance indicators (SPIs) with the appropriate grade-level cluster, language domain, and topic. Every strand of SPIs illustrates content-related language at five levels of English language proficiency, thus providing examples of language targets that will be useful for students to learn at each level of language proficiency.

As previously emphasized, each element of a sample performance indicator—language function, topic, and support—represents a range of possibilities. Because of this flexibility, teachers can shape the SPIs through transformations of selected elements to meet the needs of their students and language education programs. In addition to helping teachers differentiate instruction, this flexibility means that educators can maximize connections to state, district, and school curricula.

Depending on the amount of time devoted to a lesson and the scope of instruction, one or more SPI transformations may be necessary. The depth of study determines in part which transformations apply as well as the kinds of activities, tasks, or projects the students will engage in. Although a single lesson may contain just one activity, instructional units or themes often include student projects involving multiple tasks and activities. Thus, teachers may need to carry out a number of transformations on the targeted strands. The need to align instruction with district and state requirements will also guide decisions about transformations. Here are several questions to ask in approaching Step 3:

- How much time will be devoted to this unit of instruction? Will it include one lesson or multiple lessons?

- How many classrooms and teachers will be involved?

- Which language domains will be addressed?

- What district requirements or state academic standards need to be addressed?

Step 4: Develop language objectives.

The content students need to learn provides the anchor and context for language development. There is no definitive number of prescribed language objectives for any lesson or unit; ideally, language and content teachers should work together to identify the language students need to learn in order to access the content knowledge. *Content objectives* represent the knowledge and skills of the content-area topic, whereas *language objectives* center on the language requisite for accessing that content and demonstrating learning. Although there may be a uniform set of content objectives for all the students in a class, language objectives should be developed according to the students' levels of English language proficiency.

Step 5: Differentiate instructional activities according to levels of language proficiency.

The strands of SPIs provide examples of language tasks related to a range of content topics at specific proficiency levels and within grade-level clusters; thus, they are a starting point for planning differentiated instruction. The task descriptions offer a model for generating additional tasks appropriate for students at varying proficiency levels. As teachers plan instructional units, the strands of SPIs can guide the design of language-focused activities such as developing vocabulary, practicing sentence patterns, and drafting content-based texts. These differentiated instructional activities widen the range of communicative functions for all students at each level of language proficiency in the class.

Differentiation does not mean lowering expectations for student performance. Rather, it means providing access to the content from different perspectives or routes, so that all students in the class can learn and participate in the lesson. Lessons can be differentiated in various ways. Rothenberg and Fisher (2007) identify three ways of differentiating instruction:

- through sources: the materials and other resources students use to access the content

- through process: the strategies, activities, and structures students use to learn the content

- through products: what students do to show they have learned the content

These three categories cover the spectrum of instructional planning and illustrate how extensively, or narrowly, lessons can be differentiated to meet students' needs.

Step 6: Plan for instructional supports.

An important component in planning instruction for English language learners is the use of supports. Supports provide a mechanism for scaffolding learning as students are developing their language skills and when those skills are being assessed. Because supports play a critical role in language instruction and assessment, they are embedded within the sample performance indicators at ELP Levels 1–4. These supports fall into three categories: visual, graphic, and interactive. Figure 4.9 lists examples of each type of support for reference in creating instruction and assessment activities appropriate for students' language proficiency levels.

Using the information he had collected about his English language learners, Michael began the process of tailoring the social studies curriculum to his students' language needs. In collaboration with Rachel, he decided to develop a thematic, integrated unit of instruction on Mesoamerican and Andean civilizations that would last 2–3 weeks. Michael and Rachel reviewed the TESOL ELP standards to find a strand of SPIs that modeled the academic language related to this topic across proficiency levels. They chose the strand of SPIs shown in Figure 7.2, related to the language domain of writing, noting its reference to the Aztec and Mayan cultures.

As they prepared, Michael and Rachel kept in mind that the majority of the linguistically and culturally diverse students at their school were of Mexican descent, so they could serve as both cultural envoys and resources for other students during this unit. In addition, because the topic came from the existing curriculum, teachers in the building had, over the years, accumulated related materials in both English and Spanish that were available for student use.

Because the English language learners would need to develop both oral language and literacy skills for this unit, Michael and Rachel transformed the writing strand of SPIs to include the other language domains of listening, speaking, and reading. The result was a theme-based matrix for Standard 5, illustrated in Figure 7.3.

Grade-level cluster: 6–8
Standard 5: The language of social studies
Language domain: Writing
Topic: Cultural perspectives and frames of reference

Level 1	Level 2	Level 3	Level 4	Level 5
List characteristics of people, places, or time periods using visual or graphic cultural references	Describe people, places, or time periods using visual or graphic cultural references (e.g., map of Southeast Asia or artifacts from Ming Dynasty)	Compare/contrast people, places, or time periods using visual or graphic cultural references (e.g., Aztec, Mayan, and Egyptian pyramids)	Give detailed examples of cross-cultural connections among people, places, or time periods using visual or graphic cultural references	Defend and provide support for cross-cultural perspectives

Figure 7.2. A Strand of Sample Performance Indicators From Standard 5, the Language of Social Studies. Adapted from *PreK–12 English Language Proficiency Standards* (TESOL, 2006, p. 87).

Grade-level cluster: 6–8
Standard 5: The language of social studies
Topic: Cultural perspectives and frames of reference

Domain	Level 1	Level 2	Level 3	Level 4	Level 5
L I S T E N I N G	*Find examples of people, places, or time periods based on illustrations or authentic materials and oral commands*	*Identify people, places, or time periods described orally using visual or graphic cultural references*	*Create representations of people, places, or time periods based on oral directions using visual or graphic cultural references and models*	*Role-play people, places, or time periods based on oral stories using visual or graphic cultural references*	*Evaluate delivery of oral presentations on cultural references to people, places, or time periods*
S P E A K I N G	*Name and share artifacts or references from native cultures (in L1 and L2) in small groups*	*Describe artifacts or references from native cultures (in L1 and L2) in small groups*	*Tell stories from native cultures using artifacts or cultural references in small groups*	*Present oral reports on cultural references to people, places, or time periods in small groups*	*Give multimedia presentations on cultural references to people, places, or time periods*
R E A D I N G	*Match words or phrases to people, places, or time periods using visual or graphic cultural references with a partner*	*Categorize phrases or sentences related to people, places, or time periods using visual or graphic cultural references with a partner*	*Arrange sentences on cultural references to people, places, or time periods using visual or graphic support*	*Interpret paragraphs on cultural references to people, places, or time periods using visual or graphic support*	*Infer cultural references to people, places, or time periods using modified grade-level text*
W R I T I N G	List characteristics of people, places, or time periods using visual or graphic cultural references	Describe people, places, or time periods using visual or graphic cultural references (e.g., map of Southeast Asia or artifacts from Ming Dynasty)	Compare/contrast people, places, or time periods using visual or graphic cultural references (e.g., Aztec, Mayan, and Egyptian pyramids)	Give detailed examples of cross-cultural connections among people, places, or time periods using visual or graphic references	Defend and provide support for cross-cultural perspectives

Figure 7.3. A Theme-Based Matrix Created Through Transformation of a Strand of SPIs.

In developing the language objectives for the unit, Michael and Rachel focused on the students' levels of English language proficiency. They planned to build on students' prior experiences and the language to which they had previously been exposed. To clarify their expectations for student performance at each ELP level, they reviewed the performance definitions for the five levels of English language proficiency in the TESOL standards matrix (see Figure 3.1).

Next, Michael and Rachel considered what language the English language learners would need to access the unit content; in particular, what language was associated with location of places, identification of characteristics and contributions, and time frames. They chose from a range of possibilities, given the target content, their knowledge of the students' needs and proficiency levels, and the requirements of the tasks they had designed for the unit.

Michael and Rachel collapsed the listening and speaking strands of SPIs from their theme-based matrix into a set of objectives for oral language development, and they merged the reading and writing strands into objectives for literacy development. Their differentiated, yet scaffolded, language objectives for the unit unfolded as follows:

	Objectives for Oral Language Development of English Language Learners
ELP Level	Objective
1	Distinguish between _this_ and _these_ using concrete referents
2	Use descriptive language with _this_ and _these_ in context of Aztec, Incan, or Mayan cultures (such as in describing artifacts or locations)
3	Use sequential language in describing artifacts, people, places, or stories from Aztec, Incan, or Mayan cultures within a specified time frame
4	Use transitional language in presenting oral reports on artifacts, people, places, or stories from Aztec, Incan, or Mayan cultures

Objectives for Literacy Development of English Language Learners	
ELP Level	_Objective_
1	Match _this_ and _these_ to words/phrases about characteristics of Aztec, Incan, or Mayan cultures and sort accordingly
2	Produce or reproduce descriptive language about artifacts, people, or places of Aztec, Incan, or Mayan cultures
3	Use comparative language to contrast artifacts, people, places, or time periods of Aztec, Incan, or Mayan cultures
4	Use evaluative language to select and defend one ancient Mesoamerican or Andean culture

Because the students were at more than one language proficiency level, Michael and Rachel planned to differentiate the language activities according to ELP Levels 1–4. For Level 5 students, who were approaching parity with their English-proficient peers, differentiation would be minimal—perhaps consisting of tasks requiring them to evaluate information or support a point of view. In envisioning the content for this thematic unit on Aztec, Incan, and Mayan cultures, Michael and Rachel examined not only the strands of SPIs but also the state academic content standards. Then they listed some content-related tasks students could do in this unit:

Tasks

Locate places where the Aztec, Incan, and Mayan cultures existed

Identify the characteristics and contributions of Aztec, Incan, and Mayan cultures

Trace the time frames of the rise and fall of these cultures

Once Michael and Rachel had decided on instructional activities based on the language objectives, they found the process of choosing types of support for students' language development fairly straightforward. English language learners from Levels 1 through 4 would benefit from visual, graphic, and interactive supports. Michael and Rachel's choices for the unit included the following supports:

Task 7.3. Incorporating Language into Lesson Design

Review a recent lesson you used with your students. Answer these questions to help you decide whether or not the lesson incorporated a focus on language:

- Did you identify the academic language students needed to learn in order to participate in the lesson?

- Did you design language objectives?

- How closely did the lesson's objectives align with students' language proficiency levels?

- Did students at different proficiency levels engage in the same activities, or did you differentiate instruction?

Reflecting: Is language learning taking place? How do we know?

The reflecting phase focuses on examining the effectiveness of the language instruction that has been planned and implemented to meet the needs of English language learners in the classroom.

Step 7: Review evidence of language learning and decide next steps.

In order to decide if any instructional program meets students' needs, teachers must take a critical look at information collected over time to determine whether or not students are learning. A detailed examination of how to implement standards-based assessment is presented in chapter 10. Our reason for including this step here is to emphasize that it is not enough to design and deliver instruction. Teachers must also determine whether their instruction meets and continues to meet students' language development needs. This purpose is particularly salient in the climate of accountability pervading schools across the United States. English language learners must demonstrate progress in developing English language proficiency. By tracking language development via assessments and using the ELP standards as a set of stable criteria to describe that progress, teachers and program administrators can keep track of instructional and program effectiveness and ensure that students are meeting the school's and their own targets for achievement in language development.

As his students worked on the activities in this unit, Michael collected evidence of their language learning. He observed students as they participated in various tasks and used a rating scale to indicate their progress in meeting the unit's language objectives. Michael created a form to record these ratings, organized by his students' levels of English language proficiency. The form also had room for anecdotal notes about students' language output. The following excerpt from Michael's form shows samples of his entries:

Date: _____   Class: _____

Student Name	ELP Level	Oral Objective	Literacy Objective	Comments
Hue	2	+	✔	Needs to work on artifact vocabulary
Fernando	2	+	+	His hard work is paying off
Luis	4	+	+	May want to consider him for next level
Carmen	4	✔	+	Needs more practice using transitional language

Key: 0 = no evidence   ✔ = showing progress
+ = attained objective

After Michael and his students had completed their unit on Mesoamerican and Andean civilizations, Michael reviewed his notes with Rachel, and they discussed whether any activities needed to be adjusted or lessons reframed. Together they used the TESOL ELP standards to describe the students' developing English proficiency.

Reflect and Respond

In this chapter, we examine a model for incorporating language development based on the ELP standards into curriculum and instructional planning. This standards-based language curriculum framework provides a process to guide the design of instructional activities, tasks, and projects that will support students in acquiring both social and academic English. Use the unit-planning guide in Appendix H, based on the language curriculum framework, to review your own process for planning lessons for English language learners in your classroom.

Vignette Revisited

Michael felt very pleased with the collaborative relationship that he and Rachel had developed. She had helped him to understand how his instructional plans could address the development of standards-based, grade-level content while simultaneously building language skills. Rachel's knowledge of lexical, semantic, and discourse skills appropriate for each language proficiency level had given Michael more realistic expectations for his English language learners, and he felt better able to help them build the academic language they needed to access meaningful grade-level content. Additionally, he and Rachel had worked closely with the school's curriculum team to infuse the ELP standards into the school-wide curriculum model. Michael believed that this would benefit not only the English language learners in the school but also his teacher colleagues, as they became more sensitive to and knowledgeable about the linguistic needs of English language learners.

Chapter 8
Connecting the English Language Proficiency Standards to Instructional Approaches in Elementary Classrooms

Shoot for the moon. Even if you miss,
you'll land among the stars.

—Les Brown

Guiding Question

➤ **How can educators apply the standards-based language curriculum framework to elementary classrooms?**

Vignette

Ralph Nelson took a deep breath. In a few weeks he would be starting a new math unit with his third graders. The previous year he had felt very pleased after implementing this statistics unit. It began with a lesson called "Our Names: Valuable Vowels," in which the students created bar graphs using discrete data sets. Now, however, Ralph felt a bit apprehensive. This year he had six English language learners in his class—including Arturo, a brand-new student. How could he embark on his bar graphs lesson and the rest of the statistics unit with this mix of students?

Ralph's concerns are not unique. Most teachers face these types of quandaries when they begin a new unit and also throughout the year, as new students join their classrooms. In this chapter, we illustrate how elementary-level teachers can design instructional activities that take into account the characteristics and language needs of English language learners through the implementation of the standards-based language curriculum framework introduced in chapter 7. Appendix I contains a step-by-step checklist to assist educators in implementing the standards-based language curriculum framework.

The largest numbers of English language learners enrolled in U.S. classrooms are at the elementary school level. It is during the elementary years that the academic base for success in school is established. Without strong oral language and literacy development, students are ill-prepared for the challenges awaiting them in the upper grades. To illustrate how teachers can help children develop the academic language proficiency needed for academic achievement, we show how the language curriculum framework discussed in chapter 7 can be implemented in an elementary classroom. This chapter addresses each step in the three phases of the framework: previewing, planning, and reflecting.

Previewing: What is the context for language instruction?

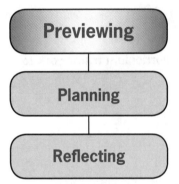

In the previewing phase, we define the parameters for implementing the English language proficiency standards based on *who* our English language learners are and *what language* is required by the content and the instructional activities for engaging students in learning that content.

Step 1: Determine English language learners' current language profiles.

All English language learners share one common characteristic: They are learning English as a second, third, or even fourth language. Often, however, this is all they have in common; these students may have very different backgrounds, experiences, abilities, and interests. Some may come with strong literacy skills in their first language, so their transition into the academic setting will most likely be smoother than that of children who come with little schooling or from places overwhelmed by war or natural disaster. Knowing what resources and needs students bring to school is a very important first step in planning and conceptualizing instruction.

Ralph already had a clear idea about the English language proficiency levels of his more established English language learners: Max, Marisa, Tien, Bouzid, and Oksana. Arturo, his newcomer student, was a different matter altogether. Although Ralph had received Arturo's initial placement score on the state English assessment, he was uncertain about how much English he could expect from Arturo, particularly in terms of this new math unit.

In order to more clearly see the abilities, needs, and characteristics of his English language learners, Ralph made a chart listing relevant details about each student (see Figure 8.1).

English Language Learner	Most Recent Test Scores (ELP Level)						Country of Origin and Native Language	Personal Characteristics
		1	2	3	4	5		
Arturo	L	X					Peru	very talented in the arts (drawing, sculpting)
	S	X						shy and quiet
	R	X					Quechua (any Spanish???)	math skills???
	W	X						
Max	L	X					Colombia	works well with others
	S		X					progressing in math but has gaps in his knowledge
	R	X					Spanish	
	W		X					
Marisa	L		X				Mexico	IEP (cerebral palsy: physical & occupational therapy for gross and fine motor skills; speech & language therapy)
	S			X				
	R	X					Spanish	
	W	X						math is not her favorite subject!
Tien	L		X				Vietnam	quiet, studious
	S		X					good computational skills
	R		X				Vietnamese	
	W	X						
Bouzid	L			X			Algeria	motivated, studious, helpful
	S				X			excels at math, especially problem-solving
	R			X			Arabic & some French	
	W				X			
Oksana	L				X		Ukraine	prefers to work with girls
	S					X		enjoys math
	R				X		Russian & Ukrainian	
	W				X			

Figure 8.1. English Language Learners' Profile Form.

Ralph also looked at the performance definitions of the five levels of English language proficiency (see Figure 3.1) to refresh his memory about what English language learners at each level of language proficiency could be expected to do. Using his highlighter, he marked the key differences between proficiency levels, as shown in Figure 8.2.

Looking over all the information he had gathered about his English language learners, Ralph felt better equipped to identify his students' individual language needs based on their profiles. He then turned his attention to the content of his lesson on bar graphs (see Appendix K).

Step 2: Analyze the language demands of the content topic.

After a lesson or unit has been identified, it is time to review the materials in terms of language demands. This review may be guided by the question, What language will students need to know to access the material and to demonstrate understanding of the topic? One might be tempted to think only in terms of the types of vocabulary needed. However, as suggested in chapter 1, language functions, grammatical structures, and discourse features need to be considered as well.

Vocabulary: Words and phrases

Word knowledge is crucial to reading comprehension and academic success. Catherine Snow (2005), for example, states that middle-class third graders with educated parents know an average of 12,000 words. This knowledge increases every year, with the expectation that the students will graduate from high school with a vocabulary of 80,000 words. Clearly, English language learners need to receive deliberate vocabulary instruction to catch up with their native-English-speaking peers. Targeted vocabulary is best learned when presented in context, with definitions that use student-friendly language, and in tasks that require both oral and written usages.

Level 1 Starting	Level 2 Emerging	Level 3 Developing	Level 4 Expanding	Level 5 Bridging
English language learners can understand and use ...				
... language to communicate with others around basic concrete needs.	... language to draw on simple and routine experiences to communicate with others.	... language to communicate with others on familiar matters regularly encountered.	... language in both concrete and abstract situations and apply language to new experiences.	... a wide range of longer oral and written texts and recognize implicit meaning.
... high-frequency words and memorized chunks of language.	... high-frequency and some general academic vocabulary and expressions.	... general and some specialized academic vocabulary and expressions.	... specialized and some technical academic vocabulary and expressions.	... technical academic vocabulary and expressions.
... words, phrases, or chunks of language.	... phrases or short sentences in oral or written communication.	... expanded sentences in oral or written communication.	... a variety of sentence lengths of varying linguistic complexity in oral and written communication.	... a variety of sentence lengths of varying linguistic complexity in extended oral or written discourse.
... pictorial, graphic, or nonverbal representation of language.	... oral or written language, making errors that often impede the meaning of the communication.	... oral or written language, making errors that may impede the communication but retain much of its meaning.	... oral or written language, making minimal errors that do not impede the overall meaning of the communication.	... oral or written language approaching comparability to that of English-proficient peers.

Figure 8.2. Key Differences Between the Levels of Language Proficiency. Adapted from *PreK–12 English Language Proficiency Standards* (TESOL, 2006, p. 39).

With a copy of the lesson plan in front of him (see Appendix K), Ralph produced a list of crucial words that he thought might be unknown to his English language learners. As he considered confusing points in the lesson, Ralph decided to change the type of data to be collected. Why should his students collect data on vowels and consonants in names, a topic that could hinder their understanding of the mathematical concepts they needed to learn, when they could collect data on something more concrete, like eye color? Ralph was convinced that his English language learners would experience more success this way. Next, Ralph thought about the words and phrases he himself used when teaching his students this topic and wrote them down on a pad of paper.

After that, Ralph began to sort both groups of words into everyday, instructional, and academic vocabulary. Within these categories he could see subgroups that made it easy for him to think about the vocabulary without having to be a linguistics expert. When he had finished sorting the vocabulary words to his satisfaction, Ralph had compiled the following lists:

Everyday Vocabulary

<u>adjectives</u>: *different, same*

<u>adverbs</u>: *together*

<u>general terms</u>: *the names of the numbers 1–25, the names of various colors, count up, eye(s), total*

<u>interrogatives</u>: *how, how many, what, which, who*

<u>tools</u>: *crayons, index cards, markers, pencils, pens, tape*

Instructional Vocabulary

<u>commands/imperatives</u>: *get into groups, get out a _____, hand in _____, copy, label, record, date, analyze, compare, contrast, organize, display, type, write, draw*

<u>general</u>: *group, partner*

---

general (not directly associated with a specific content area)

- _nouns: computer, orientation, projector, screen, title, volunteer_

- _adjectives: alike, longest, horizontal, shortest, vertical_

specialized (associated with a specific content area: math)

add, axis, bar graph, calculate, calculation(s), data, data set, data table, grid paper, highest value, label, lowest value, measure, number of, subtract, value, sum, total, difference, height of bar

technical (associated with a specific content-area topic: statistics)

bimodal, mode, range, spread

Satisfied that he had tried his best to identify pivotal vocabulary and accepting that he was learning a new process, Ralph went on to analyze the grammar forms in his bar graphs lesson.

Grammar

Once again Ralph began by looking at the lesson outline, this time for language patterns or structures at the sentence level. He underlined the sentence patterns or structures that appeared frequently. Ralph then considered his own oral language. Were there any patterns he consistently used when speaking to his students? Were there any patterns he expected his students to use when speaking to himself or other students? He gradually compiled the following lists:

Student Language:

1. _I don't understand (how to)_ _____.

2. _What does_ _____ _mean?_

3. _Can you help me, please?_

4. _____ _students have_ _____ _eyes. (number; color)_

5. _I would like to_ _____.

Teacher Language:

1. How many students have _____ eyes? (color)

2. Students/class, right now I want you to _____.

3. You have _____ minutes to finish _____.

4. Students with _____ eyes, stand over there. (color)

5. Which category of eye color had the _____ number of students? (greatest/least)

6. _____ is _____. (vocabulary word; definition)

7. Return to your seats, please, and take out _____.

8. This is a _____. (definition)

9. I need a volunteer to _____.

10. What can you tell me about _____?

11. How are _____ alike? How are _____ different?

12. What if _____ happened? (use of subjunctive)

13. What would happen to the _____? (use of subjunctive)

14. How would _____ change if _____ happened?

Ralph realized that he could only speculate about the language used for this lesson. His list would change depending on the English language proficiency level of each year's group of students, the curriculum he was using, and his own type of "teacher talk."

Discourse

Moving on to the discourse level, Ralph identified the various language skills that students would need in order to understand concepts and express their understanding during this lesson and throughout the statistics unit. For example, he reviewed how his textbook, tests, and other materials used language at the paragraph and global levels. He also returned to the analysis of his own oral discourse style and realized that he would need to carefully model specific patterns and formats for his students. Ralph made the following notes.

1. *using bar graphs*

   a. *showing how to convert numerical values from one system of symbols (numbers) to another (representational bars)*

   b. *labeling the parts of a bar graph (bars, axes, labels, title, etc.)*

   c. *interpreting and explaining the meaning of bar graphs in a coherent and cohesive manner in both oral and written forms*

2. *calculating/explaining/applying*

   a. *describing how to calculate mode and range*

   b. *explaining the differences and similarities between data sets and graphs with different orientations*

   c. *applying information about mode and range to new data sets*

Task 8.2. Listening to Your Own Language

Locate a videotape recorder or a digital recording device. During a content-area lesson, casually activate the device. Later, listen to the lesson to discover more about your personal use of oral language (i.e., your own type of "teacher talk") during content-area instruction. Think about the following questions:

- What opportunities did students have to hear and produce academic language?

- How did you model the kind of language you wanted students to use?

- What kinds of instructional supports did you use?

- Did all students participate in the lesson/activity?

Task 8.3. Analyzing the Language in a Lesson You Plan to Use

Pick a content-area lesson that you enjoy teaching and your students have enjoyed learning. Starting with the textbook and moving to supplemental material and your own "teacher talk," analyze the vocabulary, grammar, and discourse the lesson contains. Make lists of vocabulary, grammar, and discourse structures similar to Ralph's lists.

Planning: How is language incorporated into lesson design?

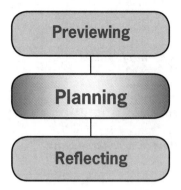

As we move from previewing to planning, we address the following steps in the standards-based language curriculum framework: matching English language proficiency (ELP) standards to language demands and transforming them as necessary, developing language objectives, differentiating instruction according to language proficiency levels, and planning instructional supports for learning.

Step 3: Match ELP standards to language demands, and decide whether and which transformations are necessary.

After identifying the language needs of students and the language demands of the lesson or unit, it is time to review the ELP standards matrices to select applicable language domains (i.e., listening, speaking, reading, and writing) and strands of sample performance indicators (SPIs). Then decisions must be made about whether and which transformations may be necessary.

Ralph recognized that his analysis of the bar graphs lesson had produced many more language demands than he could reasonably address over the course of one unit, let alone one lesson! It was time to narrow his focus. He reviewed his extensive lists from Step 2 and highlighted what he considered to be the most important language targets, so that he could plan how to support and teach them.

Paging through his dog-eared copy of PreK–12 English Language Proficiency Standards, Ralph located the matrix for Standard 3, the language of mathematics, under grade-level cluster 1–3 (TESOL, 2006, pp. 62–63). Thinking about his lesson, Ralph narrowed his focus to the strand of SPIs listed for the writing domain (see Figure 8.3).

Ralph was aware that transformations involved tinkering with any component of a cell in the standards matrices. He knew that he could alter any element of an SPI to match the appropriate grade level, language domain, topic, language functions, and instructional supports. Ralph decided that, for this lesson, he could readily substitute the topic of bar graphs for two-dimensional shapes.

Keeping his lesson plan in mind, Ralph began to transform the strand of SPIs and differentiate his expectations for the English language learners in his class. Figure 8.4 shows the result of his transformation, or substitution of topic.

Grade-level cluster: 1–3
Standard 3: The language of mathematics
Language domain: Writing

Topic	Level 1	Level 2	Level 3	Level 4	Level 5
Two-dimensional shapes	Label shapes of everyday, real-life examples	Generate lists of everyday illustrated examples of shapes (e.g., rectangles: windows, doors, books)	Describe features of everyday illustrated examples of shapes (e.g., "A door has four sides.")	Create descriptive paragraphs using features from everyday illustrated examples of shapes	Produce stories using features from everyday examples of shapes

Figure 8.3. A Strand of Sample Performance Indicators From ELP Standard 3 (Topic: Two-Dimensional Shapes). Adapted from *PreK–12 English Language Proficiency Standards* (TESOL, 2006, p. 63).

Step 4: Develop language objectives.

Whereas content objectives represent knowledge and skills, language objectives focus on the language required for accessing that content and demonstrating learning. One way of determining language objectives is to ask the question, What language do students need in order to complete the required tasks during content-area instruction?

Grade-level cluster: 1–3
Standard 3: The language of mathematics
Language domain: Writing

Topic	Level 1	Level 2	Level 3	Level 4	Level 5
Bar Graphs	*Label bar graphs using everyday examples*	*Generate a list of words that describe information in bar graphs*	*Describe information in bar graphs using phrases and short sentences*	*Create descriptive paragraphs using information in bar graphs*	*Produce stories using information in bar graphs*

Figure 8.4. A Strand of SPIs Created for a Math Unit Through Transformation of Topic. Adapted from *PreK–12 English Language Proficiency Standards* (TESOL, 2006, p. 63).

Ralph's English language learners fell into two groups: those at the early stages of second language development (ELP Levels 1 and 2) and those who were midway along the path to full English language proficiency (Levels 3 and 4). Therefore, Ralph developed a separate set of language objectives for his bar graphs lesson for each group of students:

> ## Language Objectives for Writing
>
> ### Students at ELP Levels 1 & 2:
>
> *Reproduce vocabulary related to bar graphs from word/phrase walls*
>
> *Use greatest and least in phrases to describe information in bar graphs*
>
> ### Students at ELP Levels 3 & 4:
>
> *Use descriptive words, phrases, and sentences to explain information in bar graphs*

Step 5: Differentiate instructional activities according to levels of language proficiency.

Differentiated instruction is not a novel concept. Many educators no longer teach "to the middle" but adapt their instruction to meet individual students' needs, interests, and strengths. One important aspect of differentiation for English language learners is taking into account the language proficiency level of each individual student. The strands of SPIs are valuable tools for differentiating instruction because they provide examples of language activities at different proficiency levels within grade-level clusters.

With a bright highlighter in hand, Ralph went back over his lists, charts, and plans and highlighted the items he considered most necessary for comprehending the content of this lesson, in particular, as well as the whole unit and other units or content areas. Then he made a master chart of language targets, differentiated according to the language proficiency levels of his students. Ralph's master chart appears in Figure 8.5.

Step 6: Plan for instructional supports.

Instructional supports are tools to assist English language learners in communicating with others and accessing content. Supports can be visual (e.g., gestures, video clips), graphic (e.g., maps, charts), or interactive (e.g., small group discussion, think-pair-share, working with an instructional assistant). Figure 4.9 in chapter 4 provides additional examples of each type of support. When planning instruction for English language learners at the first four levels of language proficiency, the use of supports to scaffold instruction is crucial.

Target Language	Level 1	Level 2	Level 3	Level 4	Level 5
	Arturo	*Max, Marisa, & Tien*		*Bouzid & Oksana*	
Vocabulary	*bar graph, grid paper, longest, shortest*	*all of Level 1, plus the following: axis, same, different, orientation*		*all of Levels 1–3, plus the following: calculate, mode, range, value, horizontal, vertical*	
Language Functions	*copy, label*	*describe*		*create, describe, explain*	
Grammar	*Practice using this sentence frame: "This is a _____."*	*Produce answers using this format: "_____ students had _____ eyes."*		*Use comparative structures such as <u>greater than, less than, longest, shortest</u>*	
Discourse				*Describe the mode and range of a set of data*	

Figure 8.5. Language Targets Differentiated by Language Proficiency Levels.

Some teachers have the help of a paraprofessional or instructional assistant who can work with English language learners on specific skills or tasks. To coordinate efforts between teachers and instructional assistants, a useful form is included in Appendix L.

Ralph began to brainstorm lists of different types of instructional supports his English language learners could use in this lesson and perhaps throughout the unit. Within a short period of time, he had compiled the lists in Figure 8.6.

Tired but well-satisfied with the thought he had put into planning support and instruction for his English language learners, Ralph decided to take one last look at his lesson. For future lessons he could use the assistance of Esperanza, the ELL paraprofessional, who was currently on medical leave. He really missed her, especially since Arturo's arrival. Ralph found himself envisioning how Esperanza could pre-teach some of the vocabulary and make connections to the students' previous experiences when possible. She could practice the Level 1 and Level 2 grammar objectives with Arturo, Max, and Marisa and review vocabulary in both Spanish and English. This additional support would help the English language

Level 1	Level 2	Level 3	Level 4	Level 5
• *using a teacher-prepared, illustrated bar graph* • *working with a partner* • *using index cards to practice vocabulary* • *receiving extra teacher support (perhaps teacher-led small group?)*	• *using a teacher-prepared, illustrated bar graph* • *working with a partner*	• *using a teacher-prepared, illustrated bar graph* • *working with a partner*	• *working with a partner*	• *working with a partner, if desired*

Figure 8.6. Possible Instructional Supports for English Language Learners in a Math Unit.

learners feel more comfortable during the actual lesson, because they would recognize some of the vocabulary and grammar structures he would be using. Ralph let out a big sigh as he realized that he would be teaching this lesson alone.

Ralph then decided to change the Building Background / Assessing Prior Knowledge section of his lesson plan. Instead of bringing in a bar graph from a book or newspaper with vocabulary from a completely different context, Ralph decided to display an example of a graph constructed by his students the previous year. Although the topic of that graph would be letters rather than eye colors, the overall similarity of the example would be helpful for his English language learners.

Reflecting: Is language learning taking place? How do we know?

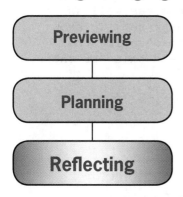

In implementing the last phase of the language curriculum framework, reflecting, we interpret the data on language that have been collected over time and figure out how the information can best be used. Reflection is intended for teachers and students alike. A wide and varied range of strategies may be applied to determine the extent of language learning. The choice often depends on how teachers craft and deliver instruction and assessment, the influence of school or district policy, and the extent to which students are involved in monitoring their own progress in language development.

Step 7: Review evidence of language learning and decide next steps.

Assessment is an ongoing process for determining the current level of a student's knowledge and performance. A central feature of effective teacher-based assessment is a strong link between assessment and instruction, with one informing the other. Teachers like Ralph understand the cyclical nature of this process, which involves setting learning goals, collecting data, interpreting the data, and setting new goals.

Finally, taking into account the instructional changes he had planned, Ralph considered the assessment portion of the lesson (see Appendix K). Based on his language targets, Ralph developed a descriptive rubric for Levels 3 and 4 and a checklist for observing language development for Levels 1 and 2. He then changed his assessment choices to the following:

1. Provide each student with a new sheet of grid paper. Instruct students to collect, organize, analyze, and display data on the eye colors of at least five family members or friends. To demonstrate their skills and knowledge of the content, students are to include a data table and both orientations of bar graphs, as well as calculations of the mode and range for the data set. To show their English language development, students are to use appropriate vocabulary, grammatical structures, and discourse on bar graphs according to their levels of English language proficiency.

2. Provide each student with a teacher-prepared list of 20 names and eye colors and a new sheet of grid paper. Instruct students to analyze, organize, and display data on eye colors. To demonstrate content knowledge, students are to include a data table and both orientations of bar graphs, as well as calculations of the mode and range for the data set. To show English language development, students are to describe the process, explain their calculations, and give details of their results in oral or written form.

Task 8.4. Ways of Pre-Teaching Content-Area Language: Vocabulary, Language Functions, Grammar, and Discourse

Brainstorm possible strategies to assist your students in learning new or difficult terms, phrases, and structures before a lesson is taught. Some ideas include word walls, concept maps, cognates, and formulaic phrases. If you have an instructional assistant, consider the ideas Ralph envisioned for Esperanza. Select one or two pre-teaching activities from the list, and implement them in your classroom over a span of 3–4 weeks. Then use a variety of assessments to determine whether those strategies are working.

Reflect and Respond

This chapter illustrates how the English language proficiency standards can be connected to instruction in an elementary classroom. It also shows how to plan for instruction and assessment using the standards-based language curriculum framework introduced in chapter 7.

As you plan your next lesson or unit, use the standards-based language curriculum framework checklist in Appendix I for guidance in constructing a meaningful lesson that addresses both the content and the language targets for your English language learners.

Vignette Revisited

Carrying out this recursive process of planning a lesson—creating differentiated content and language objectives and reviewing his lesson plan prior to teaching—had shown Ralph that as his ideas and skills in teaching English language learners continued to evolve, so, too, would his lesson plans. He also acknowledged that applying the language curriculum framework would get easier with practice. In the meantime, Ralph felt a tidal wave of energy as he realized that he was doing his best to address the needs of all his students.

Chapter 9
Connecting the English Language Proficiency Standards to Instructional Approaches in Secondary Classrooms

We are continually faced with a series of great opportunities brilliantly disguised as insoluble problems.

—John W. Gardner

Guiding Question

➤ **How can educators apply the standards-based language curriculum framework to secondary classrooms?**

Vignette

Luisa Pérez, a dedicated environmental science teacher in her native Puerto Rico, wanted to continue her career upon emigrating to the mainland. The vast rain forest and other natural resources on her island had been the laboratory for much of her teaching. Through inquiry-based learning, her students had formulated hypotheses, collected data through observation and field notes, analyzed the results, and discussed their findings on issues that clearly affected their lives.

Life was much different for Luisa in the sprawling high school to which she was now assigned. She discovered that many of her students were English language learners who had not had the benefit of continuous schooling; some were political refugees from remote villages, others were immigrants helping to support their families back in their homelands, and still others had major responsibilities at home, such as caring for younger siblings. In contrast to these students who lacked a firm foundation in their native languages, she also had some English language learners who were quite literate in their native languages and had studied English as a foreign language in their home countries.

In her inaugural year at this high school, Luisa faced the daunting challenge of trying to support the English language learners in her mainstream biology classes so they could make progress in their English language development *while simultaneously reaching their biology achievement targets. She carried the added pressures of working with a preset curriculum, using assigned books for her classes, and preparing her students for the high-stakes end-of-course test. After being introduced to the TESOL English language proficiency (ELP) standards at the high school faculty orientation, Luisa decided that these standards would provide the entrée for her students into the language of science and the world of science education.*

In this chapter, we show how to build curriculum and instruction reflective of the characteristics and language needs of English language learners at the secondary level through the implementation of the standards-based language curriculum framework introduced in chapter 7. Appendix I contains a step-by-step checklist to assist educators in implementing the standards-based language curriculum framework.

➤ How can educators apply the standards-based language curriculum framework to secondary classrooms?

English language learners face a number of challenges when they enter high school. They are expected to learn grade-level content in demanding and complex subject areas while at the same time developing English proficiency and figuring out how to navigate the unfamiliar structures and practices of the high school environment. It is unlikely that their teachers will be able to provide the support these students need to meet their academic challenges because high school teachers are trained to teach content, not the academic language used to access that content. In addition, English language learners are expected to meet rigorous standards and demonstrate their achievement on high-stakes assessments designed for all students within a relatively short time span. Short and Fitzsimmons (2007) characterize the learning demands on English language learners as "double the work" (p. 1) of their monolingual peers.

If the goal of high school is to prepare students to become productive contributors to society, then the curriculum should be the stimulus for creating responsible, independent, lifelong learners. At the same time, a curriculum for English language learners has to be sensitive to these students' linguistic and cultural backgrounds and has to assist them in accessing the array of academic learning in their high school classes while maintaining their identity as teenagers and young adults.

Our language curriculum framework can be used to identify the academic language students need to develop and to incorporate it into instructional and assessment activities in secondary classrooms. This chapter addresses each step in the three phases of the framework: previewing, planning, and reflecting.

Previewing: What is the context for language instruction?

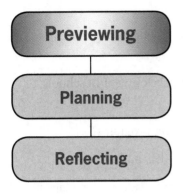

In the previewing phase, we define the parameters for implementing the English language proficiency standards based on *who* our English language learners are and *what language* is required by the content and the instructional activities for engaging students in learning that content.

In many high schools, curriculum is structured and preset. Much of the content in a course may be based on district-selected textbooks and materials, and end-of-course tests may be required in core subject areas. The school day is typically compartmentalized for teachers and students alike; it is usually divided into periods or blocks, so that planning time for instructional activities is limited. Consequently, secondary teachers have few occasions to collaborate across content areas or departments.

Secondary teachers must identify the language associated with their content areas and integrate the development of that language into the curriculum, irrespective of how that curriculum is structured. English language learners in classrooms where English is the medium of instruction often must rely on language just above their English language proficiency level to access the necessary content. For students who are highly mobile, who have had limited or interrupted formal schooling, or who are long-term English language learners, the high school curriculum is indeed a challenge.

Task 9.1. Curriculum Preview

Reflect on the curricular resources available in your school or district for secondary English language learners. Then answer these questions:

- What curricular innovations would help your English language learners?
- What constraints might impede the implementation of these innovations?
- What could you, as a language teacher, do to counteract those constraints?
- What suggestions do you have to ensure that curriculum is connected to English language learners' lives and experiences?

Step 1: Determine English language learners' current language profiles.

By examining English language learners' performance in listening, speaking, reading, and writing in various contexts and classes, teachers can formulate language profiles of their students. Information for students' language profiles can be gathered from a variety of sources, including the results of formative and summative assessments of language proficiency, student portfolios, and teachers' professional judgment. For older students, self-reported data on personal interests and knowledge of various topics (in English or the native language) may also aid in unit planning. Through analyzing students' language profiles, teachers can better match students to available language resources and instructional practices.

Here are some questions teachers may find helpful in gaining an understanding of their students' overall language development:

- Have the students had continuous opportunities for language development in schools inside and outside the United States?

- Have the students had continuity in their U.S. language education programs?

- To what extent are the students literate in their native language (L1) and in English (L2)?

- To what extent do the students have oral proficiency in social and academic language in their L1 and L2?

- What are the students' academic achievements (in L1 or L2)?

- What other school-based data (e.g., transcripts) offer information about how students fare with the language of school?

Luisa realized that her English language learners varied enormously. To get a better sense of their individual and collective language profiles, she set up a student record system on her laptop computer. First she entered information about her students that she gathered from school records such as the district's home language survey and literacy survey. (See Appendixes F and G for examples of such surveys.) From these records she learned that some of her students had attended school in their home countries and were literate in their first languages. Many others, however, had literacy skills below grade level due to their inconsistent educational experiences.

As Luisa observed her English language learners at work on various classroom tasks, she entered brief anecdotal notes to flesh out the data in her student record system. These rich descriptions would help her set high yet realistic performance expectations for the students in her class. Luisa's increased understanding of her students' language proficiency would also help her identify the challenges inherent in the textbook readings she assigned, the written tasks her students had to complete, and the time constraints for completing the work.

Task 9.2. A Language-Focused Needs Assessment

Think about how to collect information for student language profiles that would be useful for instructional planning. Consider the following questions:

- How might teachers in your school go about identifying the instructional requirements for English language learners?

- What information is currently available—such as formative, benchmark, and summative assessment data—that may identify students' language needs?

- How might teachers collect demographic and historical information pertinent to English language learners?

- How might teachers obtain self-reported data from students to gain insight into English language learners' perceptions about their own language development?

- What evidence is available from students, such as writing samples, that can provide insight into their classroom performance?

Step 2: Analyze the language demands of the content topic.

At the secondary level, English language learners face a seemingly overwhelming task because the academic language load in the content areas ratchets up dramatically. In Step 2, teachers should begin to think about the range of language features necessary for students to communicate content within a given unit. As we emphasize in chapters 1 and 2, a variety of linguistic factors—including vocabulary, grammatical structures, and discourse—make up the language demands of content tasks. Teachers should center their instructional planning on the language features that occur naturally in content lesson delivery.

The upcoming topic in the biology curriculum was ecosystems. Because the school was near a large waterway, Luisa had designed a unit on watersheds. The students would explore water quality and watershed preservation as part of stream ecology. They would also use the scientific method to measure the effects of pollution on microorganisms in the water. To help prepare for this unit, Luisa reviewed the materials she would use with her students as well as the instructional tasks they would engage in. As she did this, she focused on the language structures students would have to process and produce: the vocabulary, grammatical structures, and forms of discourse in which the content was couched.

Vocabulary: Words and phrases

First, Luisa identified focus words and phrases from the unit. Then she categorized the vocabulary as general (not directly associated with scientific study), specialized (associated with scientific study), and technical (related to the scientific topic of watersheds). The result of her efforts looked like this:

<u>General Vocabulary</u>

experiment	evidence	investigation
advice	recommendation	sequence
suggestion	analyze	interpret
gravity	branching	polluted
creek	stream	river

<u>Specialized Vocabulary</u>

hypothesis	water quality	scientific inquiry
ecosystem	nutrients	habitat
aquatic	photosynthesis	microorganisms

<u>Technical Vocabulary</u>

runoff	tributary
food web	watershed
aquatic macroinvertebrate	

Grammar

Satisfied with her vocabulary lists, Luisa next tackled the task of identifying the grammatical structures students would need to recognize and use in the unit activities and assignments. As part of their inquiry, the students would be comparing water conditions over time using data from a table on water quality. Luisa considered the kinds of sentences her students would need for this activity and wrote down three sentence patterns:

1. Conditions in Stream X are _____. (getting better / getting worse / remaining the same)

2. Stream X has _____ (better / worse / the same) stream conditions _____ (than/as) Stream Y.

3. I know this because _____.

The students would also design experiments to measure the effects of two runoff pollutants on an aquatic macroinvertebrate. They would have to write step-by-step instructions on how they had set up their experiments and also write their hypotheses. Luisa listed the kinds of sentences needed to complete this part of the unit:

1. First, _____. Second, _____. Third, _____.

2. Then, _____. Next, _____. Finally, _____.

3. I hypothesize that _____.

4. I think that _____.

Discourse

Finally, thinking about discourse-level language skills, Luisa reviewed the lab report that students would fill in to report on their experiments. Luisa realized that she would have to teach her English language learners how to formulate hypotheses using interrogatives, how to list materials, how to sequence the steps used in the experiment, and how to describe the results in the past tense.

```
Science Lab Report

Purpose:

Hypothesis:

Materials:

Methods:

Diagram of Experimental Design:

Results:

Description of Results:

Conclusion:
```

Task 9.3. A Topic's Associated Language Features

Choose a topic that is appropriate for your grade-level cluster. (Use a topic from a unit you are familiar with or refer to Appendix A.) Think about the language features required for classroom instruction and assessment of this topic.

Generate specific examples of the selected language features for this topic and categorize them as vocabulary, grammar, or discourse. Use the worksheet below to jot down your ideas.

A Topic's Associated Language Features

Grade-level cluster: _____ Topic: _____

Potential language features:

Vocabulary:

Grammar:

Discourse:

Planning: How is language incorporated into lesson design?

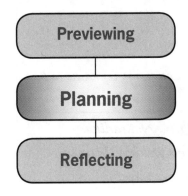

As we move from previewing to planning, we address the following steps in the standards-based language curriculum framework: matching ELP standards to language demands and transforming strands of sample performance indicators as necessary, developing language objectives, differentiating instruction according to language proficiency levels, and planning instructional supports for learning.

Step 3: Match ELP standards to language demands, and decide whether and which transformations are necessary.

Once the language demands of the lesson and the language profiles of the students have been identified, the TESOL ELP standards provide a lens for focusing on language targets at a range of proficiency levels. These targets can be used for instructional planning of the content lesson and for assessment. With the content topic in mind, teachers can examine the oral language and literacy skills that English language learners at various proficiency levels will need to participate in the tasks and activities of the lesson.

As a science teacher, Luisa concentrated on developing her students' language proficiency through ELP Standard 4, the language of science. Referring to her copy of PreK–12 English Language Proficiency Standards (TESOL, 2006), she thought about the language necessary for her English language learners to access the content of her unit as they grappled with its science concepts. Luisa chose the topic Scientific research and investigation from the standards matrix for grade-level cluster 9–12 (p. 95), because she knew it represented the "science as inquiry" strand of her state's science standards and would support the learning objectives for her unit on water quality in watersheds.

Luisa was sensitive to her students with limited or interrupted formal schooling and to new arrivals in her class, so she planned to use ELP Standard 1 (social, intercultural, and instructional language) to help these students draw on their prior knowledge and experiences. From the matrix for Standard 1 (pp. 88–89), Luisa chose the topic Strategies, which she planned to incorporate throughout the unit.

Although both topics came from the reading domain, Luisa found it important to address them by developing integrated language units. In this way, her students would engage in instructional activities that enhanced literacy development as well as building oral academic language proficiency. Thus, Luisa developed language targets in the listening and speaking domains for oral language development and in the reading and writing domains for literacy development. To record her decisions, she created the following chart.

Grade Level: 10		
Content Topic(s) From Academic Content Standards	Match to the TESOL English Language Proficiency Standards and Topics	Language Domains to Be Addressed
Cross-cutting topic: Science as inquiry _General topic_: Ecology _Subtopic_: Watersheds	_Standard 4_: The language of science _Topic_: Scientific research and investigation _Standard 1_: Social, intercultural, and instructional language _Topic_: Strategies	_Primary_: Reading and writing (literacy development) _Secondary_: Listening and speaking (oral language development)

Task 9.4. Selecting Language Targets From the ELP Standards

The decisions Luisa made in selecting possible language targets for her unit are presented as headings in the chart below. For this task, select a content topic for a specific grade level. Choose a topic that you teach, or refer to the list in Appendix A or to your state academic content standards. Next, choose the corresponding English language proficiency standard(s) at the appropriate grade-level cluster and find relevant subtopics associated with your topic. Finally, given your teaching situation, decide which language domains you plan to include in your instruction and assessment.

Grade level:		
Content Topic(s) From Academic Content Standards	Match to the TESOL English Language Proficiency Standard(s) and Topic(s)	Language Domains to Be Addressed (Listening, Speaking, Reading, Writing)

As a high school teacher, Luisa relied almost exclusively on topics from the 9–12 grade-level cluster even though some of her students had not had the requisite building blocks. To compensate for these English language learners' interrupted, inconsistent, or limited formal education, she considered how she might better serve them with grade-level curriculum, knowing that they ultimately must pass the high-stakes test to graduate from high school. Luisa came up with the following ideas: (a) collaborate with the school's language specialist to differentiate instruction of both content and language, (b) use Spanish, her native language, to introduce and reinforce key concepts to her Spanish speakers, (c) promote students' interaction with each other, pairing proficient English speakers with English language learners, and (d) find additional materials, including Web sites, to help strengthen the students' linguistic and conceptual development.

Having identified topics and language targets from the ELP standards, Luisa continued her planning for the unit on watersheds by figuring out which transformations might be necessary. First, she considered how she would use the strand of sample performance indicators (SPIs) on the topic of Scientific research and investigation (see Figure 9.1).

Grade-level cluster: 9–12
Standard 4: The language of science
Language domain: Reading

Topic	Level 1	Level 2	Level 3	Level 4	Level 5
Scientific research and investigation	Match vocabulary associated with scientific inquiry with illustrated examples	Categorize phrases and sentences descriptive of processes and products of scientific inquiry using graphic support (e.g., hypotheses, variables, results)	Sequence paragraphs descriptive of the processes and products of scientific inquiry using graphic support	Extract information on the processes and products of scientific inquiry using graphic support (e.g., lab reports)	Analyze, review, and critique explanations and conclusions from scientific inquiry using modified grade-level materials

Figure 9.1. A Strand of Sample Performance Indicators From ELP Standard 4 (Topic: Scientific Research and Investigation). Adapted from *PreK–12 English Language Proficiency Standards* (TESOL, 2006, p. 95).

Luisa decided to perform two transformations to customize this strand of SPIs. First, to align with her course curriculum, she introduced the subtopic of Water sampling and quality through an addition transformation. Then, through substitution and addition transformations, she specified visual and graphic supports—namely, the use of a test kit, T-chart, and data entry sheets. These transformations helped Luisa determine how she would include all of her students, at every level of English language proficiency, in the lesson on the ecology of a watershed. Figure 9.2 shows the result of her transformations. Changes resulting from the transformations appear in bold type; extraneous language has been removed.

Knowing that her students—especially those with lower levels of English language proficiency—would benefit from strategy instruction, Luisa had selected the topic of Strategies from the matrix for English Language Proficiency Standard 1 (see Figure 9.3). Because the language domain of this strand was reading, the same as the domain of the new strand of SPIs she had created on water quality, Luisa felt that she could use the strand without

Grade-level cluster: 9–12
Standard 4: The language of science
Language domain: Reading

Topic	Level 1	Level 2	Level 3	Level 4	Level 5
Scientific research and investigation	Match vocabulary associated with scientific inquiry **on water sampling & quality** with illustrated examples **from Web sites and word/phrase banks**	Categorize processes and products of scientific inquiry **on water sampling & quality** (such as hypotheses, variables, results) using **a T-chart**	Sequence processes and products of scientific inquiry **on water sampling & quality** using graphic support **and test kits**	**Interpret** information on the processes and products of scientific inquiry **on water sampling & quality** using **data entry sheets**	Analyze, review, and critique explanations and conclusions from scientific inquiry **on water sampling & quality** using modified grade-level materials

Figure 9.2. A Strand of Sample Performance Indicators Created for a Science Unit Through Addition and Substitution Transformations. Adapted from *PreK–12 English Language Proficiency Standards* (TESOL, 2006, p. 95).

Grade-level cluster: 9–12
Standard 1: Social, intercultural, and instructional language
Language domain: Reading

Topic	Level 1	Level 2	Level 3	Level 4	Level 5
Strategies	Preview visually supported text to glean basic information (e.g., menus, schedules, announcements)	Connect information from visually supported text to self and personal experiences	Scan visually or graphically supported text to obtain information	Skim visually or graphically supported text to confirm or verify information	Revise thinking or draw conclusions from information in modified grade-level text

Figure 9.3. A Strand of Sample Performance Indicators From ELP Standard 1 (Topic: Strategies). Adapted from *PreK–12 English Language Proficiency Standards* (TESOL, 2006, p. 89).

performing any transformations in planning how to weave strategy instruction into her lessons.

In reviewing the remaining strands of SPIs under Standard 1, Luisa noticed that the SPIs for the writing domain could be transformed to help her plan some writing and speaking activities for the unit. To create writing activities, she substituted the specific topic under study (namely, Water quality) for the generic "topics" within the original strand of SPIs. Then she added interactive support in the first (L1) or second (L2) language for ELP Levels 1 and 2, so that students could readily exchange information. The resulting strand of transformed SPIs is shown in Figure 9.4. Changes resulting from the transformations appear in bold type; extraneous language has been removed.

Next, Luisa extended the topic of Water quality to the language domain of speaking. She easily transformed the writing domain to the speaking domain so that the two strands could be integrated throughout the unit. She even found that some of the elements of the SPIs, such as use of register, could remain the same, because both writing and speaking are productive skills. Luisa's transformed strand of sample performance indicators is presented in Figure 9.5. Again, changes resulting from the transformations appear in bold type and extraneous language has been removed.

Grade-level cluster: 9–12
Standard 1: Social, intercultural, and instructional language
Language domain: Writing

Topic(s)	Level 1	Level 2	Level 3	Level 4	Level 5
Advice Suggestions Recommendations	List **key points about water quality** with a classmate **in L1 or L2**	Compare key points about **water quality** using a graphic organizer **in L1 or L2**	Produce or respond to e-mails, memos, or **letters** about **water quality** using appropriate register	Create or respond to **articles** about **water quality** using appropriate register and language forms	Compose personal correspondence about **water quality** using appropriate register and language forms (e.g., letters **to government officials,** essays)

Figure 9.4. A Strand of Sample Performance Indicators Created for a Science Unit Through Addition and Substitution Transformations (Writing Domain). Adapted from *PreK–12 English Language Proficiency Standards* (TESOL, 2006, p. 89).

Task 9.5. Focusing on Language: Transformations

Think about your instructional program and how you might approach the notion of transforming strands of sample performance indicators. Which kinds of transformations—addition, substitution, or combination—may be applicable to your English language learners if you

- create thematic units of instruction?

- integrate language domains?

- utilize specific resources for supports?

- narrow a topic to fit your curriculum?

Select a topic that corresponds to your school curriculum and grade. Find the corresponding ELP standard, and review the strands of SPIs for your grade-level cluster. Choose a strand that is appropriate to your topic. Referring to the discussion about transformations in chapter 6 and the example from Luisa's science unit, make the necessary transformations to customize this strand of SPIs for your particular context. Use the template in Appendix E to record your new strand of SPIs. Then share your transformed strand with other teachers.

Grade-level cluster: 9–12
Standard 1: Social, intercultural, and instructional language
Language domain: Speaking

Topic(s)	Level 1	Level 2	Level 3	Level 4	Level 5
Advice Suggestions Recommendations	*State* key points about water quality with a classmate in L1 or L2	*Present information* from a **graphic organizer** of key points about water quality in L1 or L2	*Offer pros and cons of issues* about water quality using appropriate register	*Discuss and summarize* articles about water quality using appropriate register and language forms	*Give a presentation* about water quality using appropriate register and language forms (e.g., **a multimedia report**)

Figure 9.5. A Strand of Sample Performance Indicators Created for a Science Unit Through Substitution Transformations (Speaking Domain). Adapted from *PreK–12 English Language Proficiency Standards* (TESOL, 2006, p. 89).

Step 4: *Develop language objectives.*

Freeman and Freeman (2002) say that teachers must adhere to four keys so that their instructional practices lead to school success for older English language learners:

1. Engage students in challenging, theme-based curriculum to develop academic concepts.

2. Draw on students' background—their experiences, cultures, and languages.

3. Organize collaborative activities that scaffold instruction to build students' academic English proficiency.

4. Create confident students who value school and value themselves as learners.

(p. 16)

We suggest an additional key: *Design and share explicit language targets, grounded in English language proficiency standards.* Adhering to this key enables teachers to create differentiated language objectives that meet the needs of their English language learners.

The language objectives of a unit define the language required to access the content that is expressed in the unit's content objectives. In this way, language objectives work together with content objectives to assist English language learners in maximizing their achievement.

Luisa wanted her students to take on the role of scientific researchers in exploring the effects of water quality on aquatic life in the local watershed. She realized that this unit was loaded with new language for all her students; in addition to unfamiliar vocabulary, students would need to use the language of scientific inquiry and language registers appropriate for both formal presentations and letters. Luisa thought about the range of her English language learners and began to list specific language objectives for the students at each proficiency level. When she was finished, her paper looked like this:

Oral Language and Literacy Objectives for the Water Quality Unit

All students:

Use technical vocabulary about water quality

Use the inquiry method while formulating hypotheses, conducting the investigation, and presenting the findings

Communicate to others the meaning of the findings on effects of pollutants on water quality

Students at ELP Levels 1–2:

Based on experimentation, match vocabulary on the characteristics of water ecosystems

Make hypotheses using comparative language

Record, sort, and present information on comparative water ecosystems using a sentence-level graphic organizer

Students at ELP Levels 3–5:

Following the steps of scientific inquiry, interpret and share information from data entry sheets on water ecosystems using cause-and-effect language

Make recommendations on local watersheds in letters to local government officials or in multimedia reports using formal register with cause-and-effect language

---

Task 9.6. Developing Language Objectives

Think about the curriculum of one specific course and the content of one unit from that course.

- Which language structures (vocabulary, grammar, and discourse) are associated with the unit's content or its content objectives?

- How might that language be differentiated according to English language learners' levels of English language proficiency?

- What suggestions might you offer content teachers to facilitate the use of language objectives alongside content objectives?

Step 5: Differentiate instructional activities according to levels of language proficiency.

Within a lesson, it is important to differentiate language activities according to students' levels of English language proficiency. Because language teachers are responsible for monitoring English language learners' progress in the four language domains, they are the primary sources in determining which vocabulary, grammatical forms, and types of discourse are most appropriate for their students at each level of English language proficiency.

The ELP standards matrices are formatted so that language differentiation is evident as students move across the continuum from Language Proficiency Level 1, Starting, through Level 5, Bridging, in each language domain. In the typical classroom setting, however, it may be difficult for teachers to differentiate language instruction for each level of English language proficiency in addition to differentiating content for all their students. One strategy to address this constraint is to form groups of English language learners within the classroom, with the composition of the groups depending on the language demands of the unit.

Luisa decided to form two groups of students for oral language instruction. The first one consisted of her recent arrivals and students with limited or interrupted formal schooling. The other group was composed of long-term English language learners or those who were at least midway along the second language acquisition continuum. For reading and writing instruction, the groups were rearranged so that the newcomers with native language literacy could draw on that background as they acquired reading and writing skills in English.

By analyzing how best to deliver instruction to her students at ELP Levels 1 and 2, using the TESOL English language proficiency standards as a starting point, Luisa felt that she could build these English language learners' background knowledge through their native languages as a means for them to gain access to the necessary science skills and concepts. So, as a supplement to the curriculum, Luisa arranged for her students to participate in World

Water Monitoring Day, "an international education and outreach program that builds public awareness and involvement in protecting water resources around the world by engaging citizens to conduct basic monitoring of their local water bodies" (www.worldwatermonitoringday.org). The program's Web site offered an instructional video/DVD in English along with test kit instructions in English, Spanish, French, Portuguese, and Chinese, so even her students at the lowest end of the English language proficiency scale could actively participate.

As she completed her preparations for the unit, Luisa listed some of the differentiated language activities and tasks she planned to use:

Some Differentiated Instructional Activities and Tasks on Water Quality

All students:

Watch video/DVD about testing water quality

Make hypotheses about water quality from local sources in English (and in the students' native languages)

Conduct experiments analyzing water samples, and report findings

Group project options:

Develop and present a multimedia report on water quality in the watershed, based on scientific inquiry

Make recommendations in writing to local officials based on results of scientific experimentation on water quality in the watershed

Students at ELP Levels 1–2:

Given steps in scientific inquiry in a graphic organizer, complete the organizer by selecting relevant characteristics of water quality from a word bank

Compare water samples, following these models:

   "Sample 1 is _____er than Sample 2."

   "Sample 1 has more/less _____ than Sample 2."

Show results of scientific inquiry in drawings, photographs, or PowerPoint slides

Students at ELP Levels 3–5:

Take notes on each step of scientific inquiry while conducting the experiment

Speculate on the impact of pollutants on microorganisms in the water samples (e.g., "I think that the contaminates in the watershed have had a negative impact on water quality.")

Offer recommendations to remedy problems with runoff contamination or ways to maintain high water quality

Luisa's list provides a bare-bones description of some of the approaches she used to engage her students. However, it doesn't include many teaching techniques that were part of her everyday instructional routine, such as modeling sentences, creating word/phrase walls, and previewing graphic organizers with the students.

From differentiated language objectives are born the activities and tasks that form the core of English language learners' instruction and assessment. For any given unit of instruction, a myriad of instructional strategies can emerge from a language curriculum framework. Figure 9.6 illustrates how the strands of sample performance indicators, representing the TESOL English language proficiency standards, are the foundation for differentiating language through language objectives and instructional assessment activities. In *Paper to Practice,* we discuss instruction and assessment in separate chapters; however, in the world of performance-based teaching, the two are often intertwined.

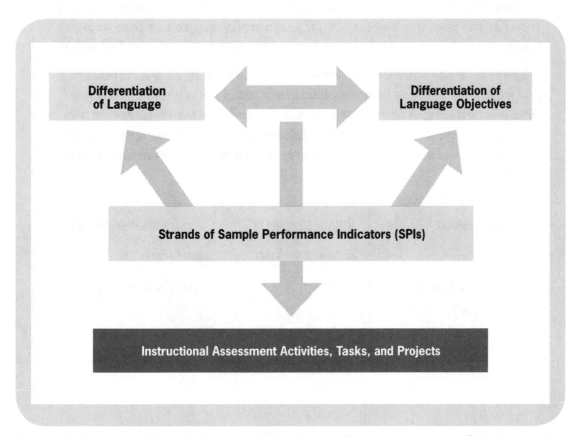

Figure 9.6. Strands of SPIs as the Basis for Differentiation of Language; Language Objectives; and Instructional Assessment Activities, Tasks, and Projects.

Step 6: Plan for instructional supports.

Supports are particularly important at the high school level, given the emphasis on complex subject-matter content. Like the other elements of the SPIs, instructional supports can be customized for individual classroom use; their purpose is to facilitate students' language development in both instructional and assessment contexts.

In preparing her unit on watersheds, Luisa was careful to include multiple types of supports for her students, knowing that her English language learners needed varied pathways and opportunities to access content through language. Because one of her goals was to promote student involvement through the exchange of information, Luisa planned to have students work with partners throughout the instructional cycle—in formulating hypotheses, conducting experiments, taking observational notes, and reporting their findings. Thus, interactive support would always be present, often combined with both visual and graphic supports to ensure that the English language learners could meaningfully engage in learning. Luisa also encouraged her students, especially those at the lower levels of English language proficiency, to use their native languages to support their oral language and literacy development in English.

Once Luisa had transformed the strands of SPIs to meet the curricular and instructional needs of her students, she listed the supports in the new SPIs and categorized them as visual, graphic, and interactive, to ensure a balanced representation. Not only would she incorporate these supports into her instruction, but she would carry them over to her assessment of in-class material.

Visual Supports	_Graphic Supports_	_Interactive Supports_
video	data entry sheets	pair work
real-life objects (e.g., test tubes, water)	T-charts	use of native language (L1)
word/phrase banks		

Reflecting: Is language learning taking place? How do we know?

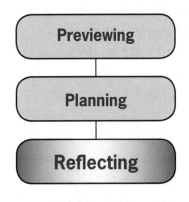

In implementing the last phase of the language curriculum framework, reflecting, we interpret the data on language that have been collected over time and figure out how the information can best be used. Reflection is intended for teachers and students alike. A wide and varied range of strategies may be applied to determine the extent of language learning. The choice often depends on how teachers craft and deliver instruction and assessment, the influence of school or district policy, and the extent to which students are involved in monitoring their own progress in language development.

Step 7: Review evidence of language learning and decide next steps.

Evidence of language learning occurs throughout the instructional assessment cycle. Teachers collect information on an ongoing basis, usually daily, by observing how their students interact and giving them instant feedback. Teachers also note the progress of their students through formative assessment during the course of a lesson and through summative assessment at the end of a unit of instruction.

> Throughout her unit on watershed ecosystems, Luisa used a variety of assessment techniques to check for evidence of language learning. She was careful to include examples from all four domains: listening, speaking, reading, and writing. As her students researched and conducted the science experiment, they had opportunities to retell or summarize each step of the procedure by keeping careful notes and summaries in their science logs.
>
> Luisa decided to create a project descriptor rubric to use for summative assessment of the unit and to serve as a student self-assessment of the various activities that constituted the final project. The rubric would guide her in monitoring instruction and serve as an anchor for describing her students' English language development.
>
> In designing the project descriptor, Luisa reviewed the transformed strands of SPIs, the language objectives, and the specific tasks and activities that pertained to the final project. She soon realized that she actually needed two rubrics, because the students had the option of presenting an oral multimedia report or composing a letter. Although the first option might be chosen by students at any ELP level, she felt that writing a letter was out of reach for her English language learners at ELP Levels 1 and 2, so she planned for the second rubric to start at ELP Level 3. Luisa's project descriptor rubrics appear in Appendixes M and N.

Luisa gave the rubrics for the final projects to her students so they would have a copy of the language targets. She carefully reviewed and explained the criteria for each project; then the students restated the criteria in their own words. In this way, Luisa shared her language expectations with the students while giving them a tool for self-monitoring and assessment.

Task 9.7. Reflecting on Language Learning

Review one of your own units of instruction. How might you better involve your students in self-assessment and reflection? What could they offer as evidence of their language learning?

Reflect and Respond

The U.S. high school is, in large part, a traditional institution and often a challenging place for English language learners—especially those who are recent arrivals, who have not previously experienced much success in school, or whose formal education has been limited or interrupted. This chapter illustrates how a standards-based language curriculum framework, easily adaptable to secondary classrooms, can connect curriculum to instruction and assessment. Think about the multistep process described in this chapter, consider how you might adapt or modify the process for your classes with English language learners, and then go try it out!

Vignette Revisited

Luisa found the TESOL English language proficiency standards to be a tremendous resource in generating ideas about the language of science and in guiding her performance-based instruction and assessment. At the same time, the standards helped her identify supports for learning, formulate language objectives differentiated according to her students' ELP levels, and share those expectations for learning with her students as they experienced science firsthand. Luisa clearly articulated the evidence her students were to produce through the activities and tasks that led to their final projects and how the language was to be evaluated against a rubric. Thus, she learned an important lesson: By using the ELP standards to identify the language her students needed to access the science curriculum, she could employ teaching strategies that had proven effective while adhering to the required curriculum and helping her students meet the academic challenges of high school.

Chapter 10
Examining Standards-Based Classroom Assessment

All assessment is a perpetual work in progress.

—Linda Suske

Guiding Questions

➤ **What is standards-based assessment?**

➤ **What are the purposes of standards-based assessment?**

➤ **How can the TESOL English language proficiency standards guide classroom assessment?**

Vignette

Heather Chu taught in a fourth- and fifth-grade mainstream classroom. Although many of her students were highly fluent in English, the class also included students at lower levels of English language proficiency. Heather had just finished a social studies unit on geographical regions in the United States. She had carefully structured the lessons so that all students could participate in the activities. She had created cooperative groups and incorporated graphic organizers into the activities. At the end of the unit, she had tested her students by giving them the chapter test from the required textbook. Although the more fluent students managed to show what they had learned, her less fluent students had performed poorly. Heather felt disappointed. She had been so sure that her carefully structured lesson would provide all of her students with rich learning opportunities! She suspected that the language used in the chapter test had interfered with her students showing what they knew about the content.

Heather wondered how she could structure assessment tasks so that students at lower English language proficiency levels could participate and demonstrate their knowledge while still meeting high standards for student performance. Perhaps, she thought, she could use the TESOL English language proficiency (ELP) standards to guide the development of assessment practices more suitable to her students' developing English language proficiency.

The TESOL English language proficiency standards provide targets for language learning and thus inform how teachers design lessons, choose materials, and adapt their teaching methods to meet their learners' language needs. However, developing instruction that draws on the ELP standards is only the first part of creating a standards-based classroom. Sound assessment practices help teachers gather and use information about how well students are developing the skills necessary to meet those standards. Assessment information offers all stakeholders—teachers, students, parents, and administrators, among others—a clearer understanding of individual student development as well as the effectiveness of instruction.

In chapter 7, we introduced a standards-based language curriculum framework to guide the development of curriculum and instruction to meet the needs of English language learners. In this chapter, we build on the third phase of this framework, *reflecting*. Specifically, we show how the TESOL English language proficiency standards can be used to create appropriate assessment practices in classrooms serving English language learners.

➤ What is standards-based assessment?

In our era of standards-based instruction and accountability, standards-based assessment affects all students. Across grade levels, students must not only learn the content of their lessons but also display this knowledge on standards-based tests of academic achievement in math, language arts, and science. English language learners have the additional task of learning the academic language needed to access the content and to demonstrate their learning. The TESOL ELP standards offer a window onto students' developing proficiency in academic language across content areas, thus highlighting areas of strength and areas for further study and development. This kind of information can guide instruction in more purposeful and effective directions so that students have greater opportunities for successfully meeting district and state criteria for accountability.

Whereas the five TESOL ELP standards cover the broad range of language competencies required for success in the classroom, the strands of sample performance indicators (SPIs) within each standard provide specific illustrations that can be used in designing assessments. These indicators show student performance at various levels of English language proficiency. They describe what students can do to demonstrate language learning related to a specific topic within an academic content area. Figure 10.1 provides an example of a strand of SPIs from Standard 5, the language of social studies. This strand shows the kinds of tasks that Heather's students might have engaged in to demonstrate their knowledge of U.S. geography.

A strand of SPIs provides a snapshot of possible student performances. In addition, it highlights the dynamic nature of learning by showing how language proficiency develops over time. When teachers use strands of sample performance indicators to develop lessons and then to assess and report student progress, they are engaged in standards-based assessment.

Standard 5: The language of social studies
Grade-level cluster: 4–5
Language domain: Speaking
Topics: U.S. regions, Topography

Level 1	Level 2	Level 3	Level 4	Level 5
State directions or locations using realia or gestures with guidance from peers	Identify features of places (e.g., "Chicago is on Lake Michigan.") using realia in small groups	Locate and describe places using realia through interaction with peers (e.g., two-way tasks)	Explore and compare locations of places using realia and other resources (e.g., the Internet) in cooperative groups	Give presentations about places using visual support (e.g., computer slide shows) in cooperative groups

Figure 10.1. A Strand of Sample Performance Indicators From ELP Standard 5 (Topics: U.S. Regions, Topography). Adapted from *PreK–12 English Language Proficiency Standards* (TESOL, 2006, p. 76).

➤ What are the purposes of standards-based assessment?

Assessment information is collected for a variety of reasons and for a range of stakeholders:

- At the classroom level, students, teachers, and parents may want to know how well individual students are progressing toward mastering specific skills. For example, are students reading at expected performance levels? Can they engage in language-dependent tasks that are part of the academic routines of specific content areas, such as writing lab reports or explaining answers to math problems?

- At the building or district level, teachers, coordinators, and principals may be interested in knowing whether the instructional approaches and materials being used are as effective as they need to be to ensure that all students have access to rich learning experiences.

- At state and national levels, schools are being held accountable for student learning, so assessment information feeds into performance models that determine whether schools are meeting expected learning goals.

Figure 10.2 illustrates this range of stakeholders and purposes for assessment.

Level of Focus	Stakeholders	Purposes
classroom	• students • teachers • parents	• allow students to assess their own progress • provide ongoing diagnostic information • create partnerships that foster communication among parents, students, and teachers • plan and improve instruction
program	• teachers • coordinators/directors • principals • counselors	• screen, place, and transition students in the program • monitor the program's progress toward student attainment of ELP standards • document student learning • improve program effectiveness
school/district	• principals • superintendents • parent advisory committees	• determine the extent to which standards have been met • guide professional development of teachers • determine effectiveness of teaching and learning • review policy based on assessment/evaluation information • allocate resources
state	• superintendents • state boards of education • business communities • state legislators	• be accountable for student learning based on attainment of standards • report summary information • create linkages with schools/districts • act on summary information and trend data
national	• U.S. Department of Education	• ensure equitable educational opportunities • determine compliance with education regulations • measure student growth toward fixed performance levels

Figure 10.2. Stakeholders and Purposes for Standards-Based Assessment. Adapted from *Scenarios for ESL Standards-Based Assessment* (TESOL, 2001, p. 11).

Task 10.1. Purposes for Assessment

Look at Figure 10.2 and identify the purposes for which you collect assessment information. Then consider the kinds of assessment information you gather. Do you feel that you're gathering enough information (and the right kinds of information) to meet your purposes? If not, what other kinds of information should you collect? How could you collect it?

➤ How can the TESOL English language proficiency standards guide classroom assessment?

Assessment is more than giving a test or using a scoring rubric. Assessment, like instruction, requires planning that takes into account a number of factors and unfolds over time. Figure 10.3 illustrates the four main steps in planning assessments that are anchored in the ELP standards. Such assessments provide critical information about student progress toward acquiring targeted standards.

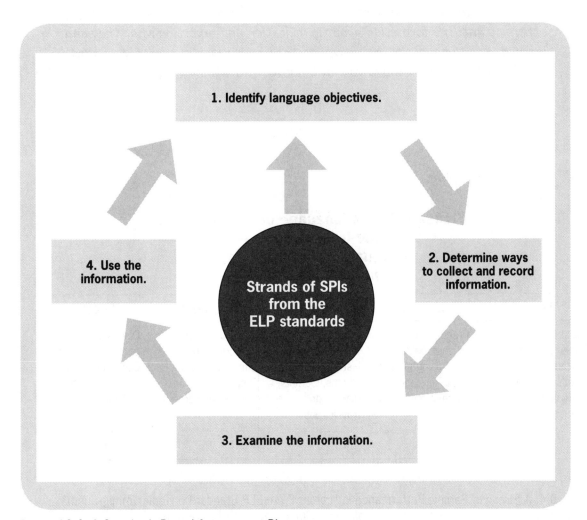

Figure 10.3. A Standards-Based Assessment Plan.

Identify language objectives.

Standards clarify what is important in student learning and act as a starting point for designing assessment plans. The sample performance indicators in the TESOL ELP standards matrices illustrate the features of academic language embedded within academic tasks and support the development of learning objectives. To begin the assessment process, then, teachers must identify which language objectives will be assessed, keeping in mind the varying language proficiency levels of students in the classroom.

Heather decided to use the ELP standards to help her plan and implement some assessment activities for her next social studies unit, which was on immigration. Heather's students ranged in English language proficiency from Level 3 to Level 5. To help them develop the language skills needed to access the social studies content, she looked carefully at the sample performance indicators for Levels 3, 4, and 5 in the strand of SPIs shown in Figure 10.4. These SPIs would guide her to identify the language skills her students needed to learn about immigration and to complete the necessary academic tasks connected to content achievement. Heather realized that all of her students would be engaged in some common learning activities, such as interviewing others to gather information about immigration and reporting what they had learned. Additional activities, as well as the way in which students displayed what they had learned, would vary by language proficiency level.

Standard 5: The language of social studies
Grade-level cluster: 4–5
Language domain: Writing
Topic: Immigration

Level 1	Level 2	Level 3	Level 4	Level 5
List family members or historical figures with countries of origin, using maps or charts	Create personal or historical family trees using graphic organizers and photographs	Produce illustrated family or group histories through albums, journals, diaries, or travelogues	Research (e.g., by conducting interviews) and report family or historical journeys	Discuss, in paragraph form, cause/effect, historical patterns, or impact of movement of peoples from nation to nation

Figure 10.4. A Strand of Sample Performance Indicators From ELP Standard 5 (Topic: Immigration). Adapted from *PreK–12 English Language Proficiency Standards* (TESOL, 2006, p. 77).

According to this strand of SPIs, students at Language Proficiency Level 5 should be able to produce expository paragraphs demonstrating their knowledge about immigration—for example, by describing historical patterns of movement or by explaining the impact of those movements. Before formulating her language objectives, Heather thought about the specific academic language features her students would need to produce these paragraphs, and she created the following list:

Level 5 Language Features

- paragraph structure (topic sentence, development, specific details)

- organizational patterns for cause/effect and sequencing events

- use of sentence connectors related to each organizational pattern (e.g., _because_, _since_, _before_, _after_)

- use of cohesion devices (reference words such as _this_, _that_, _ours_, _theirs_)

- how to create interview questions

- how to ask interview questions

- reported speech

Next, Heather studied the SPI for Level 4. It indicated that students at this level of English language proficiency should be able to conduct research and report on their findings. For the topic of immigration, they would research historical journeys, possibly ones undertaken by family members, and describe those journeys in reports. Heather listed some of the specific academic language features that Level 4 students would need to produce their reports:

Level 4 Language Features

- report format

- use of descriptive details to develop ideas

- use of an introduction and conclusion to shape the reporting

- use of sentence connectors

- how to create interview questions

- how to ask interview questions

- reported speech

Finally, Heather reviewed the Level 3 SPI. It called for students to demonstrate their knowledge about the history of a family or group through albums, journals, diaries, or travelogues. These products, less formal in structure than the language output suggested for Levels 4 and 5, would still require students to know specific academic language features. Heather's list for Level 3 looked like this:

Level 3 Language Features

- formats for personal writing, such as journals and diaries

- use of descriptive details

- story organization

- how to create interview questions

- how to ask interview questions

- reported speech

Now that she had identified the language features that her students must learn in order to accomplish their specific content tasks, Heather formulated language objectives for each level as shown below:

Language Objectives for Immigration Unit

Level 5 students: Produce cause-and-effect expository paragraphs

Level 4 students: Summarize interviews to create a report

Level 3 students: Create personal journals

Task 10.2. Identifying Language Features

Look through the standards matrices in *PreK–12 English Language Proficiency Standards* (TESOL, 2006) or the example matrices in this volume. Select one SPI from a strand and consider what academic language features you would suggest as a focus for students at that ELP level, based on the elements of the SPI. Refer to the analyses of language functions, topics, and supports in chapter 4 for additional ideas. Record your answers in the chart below.

Standard: _____

Grade-level cluster: _____

Language domain: _____

Topic: _____

ELP level: _____

SPI	Academic language features

Determine ways to collect and record information.

Checking on student progress in the classroom is a common activity for teachers as they gauge whether students are "getting it." In addition to the moment-by-moment monitoring of student engagement, however, teachers can collect and record various kinds of information about student performance that will provide useful insights about student learning.

Information collected, analyzed, and used at various points throughout a unit of instruction is called *formative* assessment. By asking students to complete self-evaluations or peer assessments, for example, teachers can gather information about how well students are able to access and use the knowledge and skills they are learning. Formative assessment supports students' ongoing linguistic and academic development as well as informs instruction. For instance, when students receive feedback on drafts of their writing, they have the opportunity to review their performance and improve it. Similarly, when teachers realize that students are struggling with some aspect of instruction, they can spontaneously insert a mini-lesson on that issue.

At the end of a unit of instruction or at the culmination of a marking period, teachers collect and record information for *summative* assessment. The form of this assessment may be the same as or similar to that used for formative assessment, but these performances are considered an end point in collecting information about student learning.

Both formative assessment and summative assessment yield useful information. However, each serves different functions in the classroom.

At this step of collecting and recording information, teachers can incorporate a great deal of creativity into the assessment process. In addition to using traditional means of assessment such as pencil-and-paper tests, teachers can gather information through performances that require students to use language to carry out tasks and activities. Students can also be active participants in assessment, providing information via self-evaluation and peer assessment. Again, the SPIs can guide the design of classroom tasks to gather assessment information.

Heather wanted to use a variety of assessment tools to check on her students' progress (formative assessment) and to determine whether her students had met the targeted levels of language use (summative assessment). Notice how she intertwined assessment with her instructional tasks.

Formative assessment

During the immigration unit, Heather observed her students as they worked to complete a variety of tasks. For example, a common task across all proficiency levels was to conduct interviews. To prepare for the interviews, her students first constructed an interview form they could use to collect information. To be successful at this task, students had to

- *form questions*

- *use language appropriate for specific interviewees*

- *incorporate vocabulary relevant to the topic of immigration*

So that students would have appropriate support, Heather paired lower level students with those at higher levels of language proficiency. To keep track of progress, she observed the partners as they prepared their interview questions. She used an observation sheet to record information on the students. Heather interacted with each pair, providing oral feedback to support the students as they worked through their tasks. At the same time, she evaluated the students: Were both partners participating? Were they able to carry out the tasks? Did they need help with vocabulary or other language demands?

When the student pairs had completed the first draft of their interview questions, they exchanged drafts with other pairs for peer review. To guide the process, Heather handed out the following peer review guide. The students had developed the items in this guide as a class, so they knew the vocabulary and format of the tool as well as how to fill it in.

Peer Review Guide			
	Yes	No	Not Sure
The questions ask for useful information.			
The questions are in the correct form.			
Immigration vocabulary is used correctly.			
Suggestions for improvement:			

Although Heather's English language learners were able to grapple with this task in English, teachers with students at lower levels of English language proficiency who share a common native language may structure classroom tasks so that students can interact with one another in their native language to clarify their understanding of the task, to have access to the academic content, or to carry out various steps of the assignment itself. In these cases, the use of the native language is an example of an instructional support.

Summative assessment

When the students had completed their final paragraphs, reports, and journals, Heather collected and assessed them using a class-designed rubric. The rubric listed specific aspects of the targeted student performance—in the case of the Level 4 students, for example, the features of the reports describing family immigration stories.

ELP Level	Academic Language Features	Evident in Student's Work (✔)

5	Expository paragraph format
	• topic sentence
	• development
	  ○ descriptive
	  ○ cause/effect
	• specific details
	• sentence connectors
	• cohesion devices
	• reported speech	

4	Report format • descriptive details • introduction and conclusion • sentence connectors • reported speech	
3	Journal/diary format • descriptive details • story organization • reported speech	

Task 10.3. Collecting and Recording Information

Choose a language objective from one of your own lessons. Brainstorm possible ways you could collect and record information about students' progress toward this objective. Consider these questions:

- Will the information serve as formative or summative assessment?

- Who will collect and record the information: you or your students?

- Are your ideas appropriate for the language proficiency level of the students?

Examine the information.

Once the information is gathered, the next step is figuring out what it means. What inferences can be made? Is additional information needed to confirm or explain what's been gathered? What patterns of growth can be seen?

The sample proficiency indicators can be used as a lens for interpreting performance as students engage in learning and assessment activities in the classroom. The SPIs also indicate the next level that teachers and students can target as the students' English language proficiency develops.

Heather had set up a record-keeping system so that she could trace the progress her students were making. She knew that she would need more than one score on one test to gain a complete picture of her students' competencies. Each piece of information would help her—and her students—understand both strengths and areas for improvement as they developed their proficiency in academic English.

When Heather was tracking whether or not students had completed a task in preparation for a more complex assignment, she often indicated student work with a checkmark (✔). At other times she included a score from a rubric or other scoring guide. Because her rubrics and other tools were geared to the SPIs and the instruction she had developed based on those SPIs, she could chart how closely each student's performance came to the targeted performance. For example, she could see whether or not the Level 4 students' reports met the criteria for a successful report.

Heather used a record log to keep track of student performance on various tasks and activities during a unit of instruction. She created the following log for her unit on immigration:

Student Name	Prepare Interview Questions	Participate in Groups	Draft Report	Final Report	Comments

Use the information.

This is a crucial step in the assessment process. At this point, information gleaned from assessment can help teachers (and others) make decisions about next steps. Are students making expected progress toward achieving a standard? Do some students need additional support? Was the unit of instruction effective, or do parts of it need to be reviewed?

Heather promoted active student involvement in learning and understood that student involvement was equally important in assessment. She made sure that all assessment information—whether teacher-gathered or collected through self-evaluation or peer assessment—was transparent for students. Her students had portfolios so they could review their language development and reflect on their strengths and areas for improvement. The portfolios offered students a clearly marked path showing their progress in attaining the ELP standards. They could also be shared with parents and other stakeholders.

Heather also monitored the assessment information so that she could track individual student growth in attaining the ELP standards. This way, she could intervene to support students as needed in specific areas. Because she collected a range of information about student performances in listening, speaking, reading, and writing, she could zero in on areas where they needed more work. When she noticed that a number of students were having difficulties in a particular area, she knew that her instruction hadn't met their needs. She used this feedback to revisit topics and develop alternative instructional approaches that might be more effective.

Task 10.4. Creating Standards-Based Assessment

How do you plan your assessments? Are they tied to ELP and academic content standards? Consider your approach to assessment and whether or not it provides information about how well your students are meeting local English language proficiency standards. Make notes about how you could follow the steps in this chapter to plan more meaningful assessments.

1. Identify language objectives.

I could . . .

_____

_____

_____

2. Determine ways to collect and record information.

I could . . .

_____

_____

_____

3. Examine the information.

I could . . .

_____

_____

_____

4. Use the information.

I could . . .

_____

_____

_____

Reflect and Respond

This chapter explores how assessment can be integrated into standards-based classrooms for English language learners. It provides a model of assessment planning that can serve a variety of purposes for collecting information about student learning. Consider how you might use this model in your own classroom. Make two lists, using these questions as starting points:

- What barriers do you face in changing how you assess your students?

- What supports are available to help you implement changes in assessment?

As you look at your lists, think about people you could work with to create changes in assessment practice. What kinds of professional development would be helpful to you?

Vignette Revisited

By using a standards-based assessment plan as part of her unit on immigration, Heather was able to more closely describe and monitor the development of her students' language skills. Even though her class contained students at several levels of English language proficiency, she was able to use a strand of SPIs from Standard 5 as a starting place to design assessment tasks appropriate to each level. These assessments helped her determine her students' progress in learning the academic language related to the material in the immigration unit, language that provided access to the academic content.

Heather's hard work in adopting a new approach to assessment paid off in several ways. She and her students—including those at lower levels of English proficiency—gained a more accurate picture of their developing language skills. Heather also became confident that she could apply these new assessment skills to other units of instruction. Although Heather realized that professional development is an ongoing process, she felt that she had taken a big step in enhancing her skills as a teacher.

Epilogue

Epilogue
Next Steps in Using the TESOL
English Language Proficiency Standards

*Education is our passport to the future, for tomorrow
belongs to the people who prepare for it today.*

—Malcolm X

Standards have become engrained in the U.S. educational landscape. For teachers and administrators throughout the country, translating standards into sound curriculum, instruction, and assessment has been an onerous endeavor. For educators devoted to English language learners, converting standards into practice has been an even greater challenge as a result of the dual focus on students' language development and their academic achievement.

Because the role of standards is substantially more complex for English language learners than it is for the general student population, we solicit support from every educator who works in a linguistically and culturally diverse school setting. We realize that the academic language and content outlined in standards tend to become entangled. For that reason, we encourage teachers to collaborate, sharing their respective expertise to create a clear and consistent pathway to academic success for English language learners.

Paper to Practice joins *PreK–12 English Language Proficiency Standards* (TESOL, 2006) as a resource for promoting standards-based education of students who are acquiring English as an additional language. Our collective work is not finished; nevertheless, with the continued effort and dedication of teachers and administrators across the country, we believe that standards can become the backdrop for high-quality, equitable, and sustainable educational programs for all students. To help advance the standards movement on behalf of English language learners, we offer the following suggestions:

- Develop a 3- to 5-year action plan for your school, program, or district that examines the influences of standards on teaching and learning for all students, with special attention to English language learners.

- Design a long-term, standards-based professional development plan in concert with your action plan.

- Formulate, adapt, or adopt a standards-based language curriculum framework, such as the one in *Paper to Practice*, to guide instruction and assessment for English language learners.

- Examine and evaluate the language education services provided by your school, program, or district in light of the characteristics of your English language learners, the implementation of English language proficiency standards, and data from formative and summative assessments.

- Create teams of language and content teachers, school leaders, and other personnel, and build in dedicated time for these team members to collaborate on educational issues relating to English language learners.

- Form a community of learners around standards-related readings and discussion of their implications for English language learners.

- Share effective standards-based instruction and assessment strategies, lessons, and units through your district's Web site.

- Maintain records and learning profiles that show English language learners' progress in listening, speaking, reading, and writing across the English language proficiency standards in relation to their academic achievement.

- Share community- and school-based native language and cultural resources with neighboring schools or districts.

- Use the TESOL English language proficiency standards as an advocacy tool to highlight what English language learners can do.

- Partner with teacher-training universities or organizations in crafting and conducting research on standards-based education of English language learners.

- Take the responsibility for educating all school personnel, as well as other stakeholders, about the language of school and how it is represented in the English language proficiency standards and the standards-based language curriculum framework.

In *Paper to Practice*, we have provided an in-depth look at the language of school as the theoretical base for the TESOL English language proficiency standards, a thorough analysis of the components of the standards matrix, and innovative suggestions for crafting standards-based instruction and assessment for English language learners through a language curriculum framework. We sincerely hope that the vignettes and examples in this book will inspire you to partner with fellow educators in expanding educational opportunities for English language learners on their pathway to academic success.

References

Works Cited

Allen, J. (1999). *Words, words, words: Teaching vocabulary in grades 4–12.* York, ME: Stenhouse.

Artiles, A. J., & Ortiz, A. A. (Eds.). (2002). *English language learners with special education needs: Identification, assessment, and instruction* (Professional Practice Series, No. 2). Washington, DC: Center for Applied Linguistics.

August, D., & Hakuta, K. (Eds.). (1998). *Educating language minority children.* Washington, DC: National Academy Press.

Baker, C. (2001). *Foundations of bilingual education and bilingualism* (3rd ed.). Clevedon, England: Multilingual Matters.

Bloom, B. S. (Ed.). (1956). *Taxonomy of educational objectives: Book I. The cognitive domain.* New York: Longman.

Cummins, J. (2005). Teaching the language of academic success: A framework for school-based language policies. In California State Department of Education, *Schooling and language minority students: A theoretico-practical framework* (3rd ed., pp. 3–32). Los Angeles: California State University Evaluation, Dissemination, and Assessment Center.

Cummins, J. (2007). Pedagogies for the poor? Realigning reading instruction for low-income students with scientifically based reading research. *Educational Researcher, 36,* 564–572.

Davison, C. (2006). Collaboration between ESL and content teachers: How do we know when we are doing it right? *The International Journal of Bilingual Education and Bilingualism, 9*(4), 454–475.

Ernst-Slavit, G., & Slavit, D. (2007). Educational reform, mathematics, and diverse learners: Meeting the needs of all students. *Multicultural Education, 14*(4), 20–27.

Francis, D. J., Lesaux, N., Kieffer, M., & Rivera, H. (2006). *Research-based recommendations for instruction and academic interventions.* Houston: Texas Institute for Measurement, Evaluation, and Statistics at the University of Houston.

Freeman, Y. S., & Freeman, D. (2002). *Closing the achievement gap: How to reach limited-formal-schooling and long-term English learners.* Portsmouth, NH: Heinemann.

Gándara, P., Maxwell-Jolly, J., & Driscoll, A. (2005). *Listening to teachers of English language learners: A survey of California teachers' challenges, experiences, and professional development needs.* Retrieved July 14, 2008, from the Center for the Future of Teaching and Learning Web site: http://www.cftl.org/documents/2005/listeningforweb.pdf

Genesee, F., Lindholm-Leary, K., Saunders, W., & Christian, D. (Eds.). (2006). *Educating English language learners: A synthesis of research evidence.* Cambridge: Cambridge University Press.

Gibbons, P. (2006). Steps for planning an integrated program for ESL learners in mainstream classes. In P. McKay (Ed.), *Planning and teaching creatively within a required curriculum for school-age learners* (pp. 215–233). Alexandria, VA: Teachers of English to Speakers of Other Languages.

Gottlieb, M. (2003). *Large-scale assessment of English language learners: Addressing accountability in K–12 settings* (TESOL Professional Papers No. 6). Alexandria, VA: Teachers of English to Speakers of Other Languages.

Gottlieb, M. (2006). *Assessing English language learners: Bridges from language proficiency to academic achievement.* Thousand Oaks, CA: Corwin Press.

Gottlieb, M., Cranley, E., & Oliver, A. (2007). *English language proficiency standards and resource guide, prekindergarten through grade 12* (2007 ed.). Madison: Board of Regents of the University of Wisconsin System on behalf of the WIDA Consortium.

Gottlieb, M., & Hamayan, E. (2007). Assessing oral and written language proficiency: A guide for psychologists and teachers. In G. B. Esquivel, E. C. Lopez, & S. G. Nahari (Eds.), *Handbook of multicultural school psychology: An interdisciplinary perspective* (pp. 245–262). New York: Lawrence Erlbaum.

Gottlieb, M., & Nguyen, D. (2007). *Assessment and accountability for language education programs: A guide for teachers and administrators.* Philadelphia: Caslon.

Graves, K. (2006). Series Editor's Preface. In P. McKay (Ed.), *Planning and teaching creatively within a required curriculum for school-age learners* (pp. v–viii). Alexandria, VA: Teachers of English to Speakers of Other Languages.

Halliday, M. A. K. (1993). Towards a language-based theory of learning. *Linguistics and Education, 5*(2), 93–116.

Hornberger, N. H. (Ed.). (2003). *Continua of biliteracy: An ecological framework for educational policy, research, and practice in multilingual settings.* Clevedon, England: Multilingual Matters.

Lacina, J., Levine, L. N., & Sowa, P. (2006). *Helping English language learners succeed in pre-K–elementary schools.* Alexandria, VA: Teachers of English to Speakers of Other Languages.

Lemke, J. (1990). *Talking science: Language, learning, and values.* Norwood, NJ: Ablex.

Marzano, R. J., Pickering, D. J., & Pollock, J. E. (2001). *Classroom instruction that works.* Alexandria, VA: Association for Supervision and Curriculum Development.

Nation, I. S. P. (2001). *Learning vocabulary in another language.* Cambridge: Cambridge University Press.

Nordmeyer, J. (2008, Winter). Delicate balance: ELL students struggle to balance language and content, while educators need partnerships and specific professional learning. *The Journal of the National Staff Development Council, 29*(1), 34–40.

Rothenberg, C., & Fisher, D. (2007). *Teaching English language learners: A differentiated approach.* Upper Saddle River, NJ: Pearson Education.

Scarcella, R. (2003a). *Academic English: A conceptual framework* (Technical Report No. 2003-1). Irvine: The University of California Linguistic Minority Research Institute.

Scarcella, R. (2003b). *Accelerating academic English: A focus on English language learners.* Oakland, CA: Regents of the University of California.

Scarcella, R., & Rumberger, R. W. (2000, Summer). Academic English key to long term success in school. *University of California Linguistic Minority Research Institute Newsletter, 9*(4), 1–2. Available from the UC LMRI Web site: http://lmri.ucsb.edu/publications/newsletters/archive.php

Schleppegrell, M. J. (2004). *The language of schooling: A functional linguistics perspective.* Mahwah, NJ: Lawrence Erlbaum.

Short, D. J., & Fitzsimmons, S. (2007). *Double the work: Challenges and solutions for acquiring language and academic literacy for adolescent English language learners.* New York: Carnegie Corporation.

Slavit, D., & Ernst-Slavit, G. (2007). Teaching mathematics and English to English language learners simultaneously. *Middle School Journal, 39*(2), 4–11.

Snow, C. (2005, July/August). From literacy to learning. *Harvard Education Letter.* Retrieved September 30, 2008, from http://www.edletter.org/current/snow.shtml

Teachers of English to Speakers of Other Languages. (2001). *Scenarios for ESL standards-based assessment.* Alexandria, VA: Author.

Teachers of English to Speakers of Other Languages. (2006). *PreK–12 English language proficiency standards.* Alexandria, VA: Author.

Tsang, S.-L., Katz, A., & Stack, J. (2008). Achievement testing for English language learners, ready or not? *Education Policy Analysis Archives, 16*(1). Retrieved January 30, 2008, from http://epaa.asu.edu/epaa/v16n1/

Vacca, R., & Vacca, J. (1999). *Content area reading.* New York: Longman.

Wiggins, G., & McTighe, J. (1998). *Understanding by design.* Alexandria, VA: Association for Supervision and Curriculum Development.

World-Class Instructional Design and Assessment Consortium. (2004). *English language proficiency standards for English language learners in kindergarten through grade 12.* Madison: State of Wisconsin. Retrieved September 29, 2008, from http://www.wida.us/standards/elp2004standards.aspx

Zwiers, J. (2008). *Building academic language: Essential practices for content classrooms, grades 5–12.* San Francisco: Jossey-Bass.

Further Reading

Academic Language

Anderson, N. J. (2005). L2 learning strategies. In E. Hinkel (Ed.), *Handbook of research in second language teaching and learning* (pp. 757–771). Mahwah, NJ: Lawrence Erlbaum.

Bailey, A. L. (Ed.). (2007). *The language demands of school: Putting academic English to the test.* Princeton, NJ: Yale University Press.

Bailey, A. L., Butler, F. A., LaFramenta, C., & Ong, C. (2004). *Towards the characterization of academic language in upper elementary science classrooms* (CSE Report No. 621). Los Angeles: University of California, National Center for Research on Evaluation, Standards, and Student Testing.

Bartolomé, L. (1998). *The misteaching of academic discourses: The politics of language in the classroom.* Boulder, CO: Westview Press.

Chamot, A. U. (2005). The cognitive academic language learning approach (CALLA): An update. In P. Richard-Amato & M. A. Snow (Eds.), *Academic success for English language learners* (pp. 87–101). White Plains, NY: Longman.

Gee, J. P. (2007). *Social linguistics and literacies: Ideology in discourses.* New York: Taylor & Francis.

Goodman, Y. (2003). *Valuing language study: Inquiry into language for elementary and middle schools.* Urbana, IL: National Council of Teachers of English.

Martiniello, M. (2008). Language and the performance of English-language learners in math word problems. *Harvard Educational Review, 78*(2), 333–368.

Richard-Amato, P., & Snow, M. A. (2005). *Academic success for English language learners: Strategies for K–12 mainstream teachers.* White Plains, NY: Longman.

Schleppegrell, M. J., & Colombi, M. C. (Eds.). (2002). *Developing advanced literacy in first and second languages: Meaning with power.* Mahwah, NJ: Lawrence Erlbaum.

Assessment of English Language Learners

Aisworth, L., & Christinson, J. (1998). *Student generated rubrics: An assessment model to help all students succeed.* Orangeburg, NY: Dale Seymour.

Alderson, J. C. (2000). *Assessing reading.* Cambridge: Cambridge University Press.

Arter, J., & McTighe, J. (2001). *Scoring rubrics in the classroom: Using performance criteria for assessing and improving student performance.* Thousand Oaks, CA: Corwin Press.

Bachman, L. F., & Palmer, A. S. (1996). *Fundamental considerations in language testing.* Oxford: Oxford University Press.

Bailey, A., & Heritage, M. (2008). *Formative assessment for literacy, grades K–6: Building reading and academic language skills across the curriculum.* Thousand Oaks, CA: Corwin Press.

Brown, H. D. (2004). *Language assessment: Principles and classroom practices.* White Plains, NY: Pearson.

Buck, G. (2001). *Assessing listening.* Cambridge: Cambridge University Press.

Butler, F. A., & Stevens, R. (2001). Standardized assessment of the content knowledge of English language learners K–12: Current trends and old dilemmas. *Language Testing, 18*(4), 409–428.

Coltrane, B. (2002, November). *English language learners and high-stakes tests: An overview of the issues* (Eric Digest No. EDO-FL-02-07). Retrieved August 27, 2008, from the Center for Applied Linguistics Web site: http://www.cal.org/resources/digest/0207coltrane.html

Darian, S. (2003). *Understanding the language of science.* Austin, TX: University of Texas Press.

Farr, B. P., & Trumbull, E. (1997). *Assessment alternatives for diverse classrooms.* Norwood, MA: Christopher-Gordon.

Fradd, S. H., & McGee, P. L. (1994). *Instructional assessment: An integrated approach to evaluating student performance.* Reading, MA: Addison-Wesley.

Genesee, F., & Upshur, J. A. (1996). *Classroom-based evaluation in second language education.* Cambridge: Cambridge University Press.

Glatthorn, A. A. (1998). *Performance assessment and standards-based curricula: The achievement cycle.* Larchmont, NY: Eye on Education.

Gottlieb, M. (1995). Nurturing student learning through portfolios. *TESOL Journal, 5*(1), 12–14.

Gottlieb, M. (2000). Standards-based, large-scale assessment. In M. A. Snow (Ed.), *Implementing the ESL standards for pre-K–12 students through teacher education* (pp.167–186). Alexandria, VA: Teachers of English to Speakers of Other Languages.

Gottlieb, M. (2008). *Assessing English language learners: A multimedia kit for professional development.* Thousand Oaks, CA: Corwin Press.

Gottlieb, M., & Boals, T. (2005). On the road to MECCA: Assessing content-based instruction within a standards framework. In D. Kaufman & J. Crandall (Eds.), *Content-based instruction in primary and secondary school settings* (pp. 145–161). Alexandria, VA: Teachers of English to Speakers of Other Languages.

Grissom, J. B. (2004). Reclassification of English learners. *Education Policy Analysis Archives 12*(36), 1–36.

Guskey, T. R., & Bailey, J. M. (2001). *Developing grading and reporting systems for student learning.* Thousand Oaks, CA: Corwin Press.

Hakuta, K., Butler, Y. G., & Witt, D. (2000). *How long does it take English learners to attain proficiency?* (Policy Report No. 2000-1). Irvine: The University of California Linguistic Minority Research Institute. Available from the UC LMRI Web site: http://www.lmri.ucsb .edu/publications/

Katz, A. (2000). Changing paradigms for assessment. In M. A. Snow (Ed.), *Implementing the ESL standards for pre-K–12 students through teacher education* (pp. 137–166). Alexandria, VA: Teachers of English to Speakers of Other Languages.

LaCelle-Peterson, M. W., & Rivera, C. (1994). Is it real for all kids? A framework for equitable assessment policies for English language learners. *Harvard Educational Review, 64*(1), 55–75.

Luoma, S. (2004). *Assessing speaking.* Cambridge: Cambridge University Press.

McKay, P. (2006). *Assessing young language learners.* Cambridge: Cambridge University Press.

Murphy, S., & Underwood, T. (2000). *Portfolio practices: Lessons from schools, districts, and states.* Norwood, MA: Christopher-Gordon.

North, B. (2000). *The development of a common framework scale of language proficiency.* New York: Peter Lang.

O'Malley, J. M., & Pierce, L. V. (1996). *Authentic assessment for English language learners: Practical approaches for teachers.* New York: Addison-Wesley.

Pierce, L. V. (2001). Assessment of reading comprehension strategies for intermediate bilingual students. In S. J. Hurley & J. V. Tinajero (Eds.), *Literacy assessment of second language learners* (pp. 64–83). Boston, MA: Allyn & Bacon.

Purpura, J. E. (2004). *Assessing grammar.* Cambridge: Cambridge University Press.

Read, J. (2000). *Assessing vocabulary.* Cambridge: Cambridge University Press.

Salvia, J., & Ysseldyke, J. E. (2004). *Assessment in special and inclusive education.* Boston: Houghton Mifflin.

Shohamy, E. (2001). *The power of tests: A critical perspective on the uses of language tests.* London: Pearson Education.

Short, D. (1993). Assessing integrated language and content instruction. *TESOL Quarterly, 27,* 627–656.

Smith, J. K., Smith, L. F., & De Lisi, R. (2001). *Natural classroom assessment: Designing seamless instruction and assessment.* Thousand Oaks, CA: Corwin Press.

Teachers of English to Speakers of Other Languages. (2000, June). *Assessment and accountability of English for speakers of other languages (ESOL) students* [Policy statement]. Retrieved August 28, 2008, from http://www.tesol.org/s_tesol/sec_document.asp?CID=32&DID=369

Valdez-Pierce, L. (2003). *Assessing English language learners.* Washington, DC: National Education Association.

Weigle, S. C. (2002). *Assessing writing.* Cambridge: Cambridge University Press.

Bilingualism, Multiculturalism, and Cultural Competence

Banks, J. A., & Banks, C. A. M. (2004). *Handbook of research on multicultural education* (2nd ed.). San Francisco: Jossey-Bass.

Bialystok, E., & Hakuta, K. (1994). *In other words: The science and psychology of second-language acquisition.* New York: Basic Books.

Carrasquillo, A. L., & Rodriguez, V. (2002). *Language minority students in the mainstream classroom* (2nd ed.). Tonawanda, NY: Multilingual Matters.

Christian, D., & Genesee, F. (Eds.). (2001). *Bilingual education.* Alexandria, VA: Teachers of English to Speakers of Other Languages.

Cloud, N., Genesee, F., & Hamayan, E. (2000). *Dual language education: A handbook for enriched education.* Boston: Heinle & Heinle.

Cummins, J. (1981). The role of primary language development in promoting educational success for language minority students. In California State Department of Education, *Schooling and language minority students: A theoretical framework* (pp. 3–49). Los Angeles: California State University Evaluation, Dissemination, and Assessment Center.

Cummins, J. (2000). *Language, power, and pedagogy: Bilingual children in the crossfire.* Clevedon, England: Multilingual Matters.

Faltis, C. J., & Hudelson, S. J. (1998). *Bilingual education in elementary and secondary school communities: Toward understanding and caring.* Needham Heights, MA: Allyn & Bacon.

Genesee, F. (Ed.). (1994). *Educating second language children.* Cambridge: Cambridge University Press.

Hymes, D. H. (1972). On communicative competence. In J. B. Pride & J. Holmes (Eds.), *Sociolinguistics* (pp. 269–293). Harmondsworth, England: Penguin Books.

Larsen-Freeman, D., & Long, M. H. (1991). *An introduction to second language acquisition research.* New York: Longman.

Lessow-Hurley, J. (2005). *The foundations of dual language instruction* (4th ed.). New York: Longman.

Lucas, T., & Katz, A. (1994). Reframing the debate: The roles of native languages in English-only programs for language minority students. *TESOL Quarterly, 28,* 537–562.

McKay, S., & Hornberger, N. H. (Eds.). (1996). *Sociolinguistics and language teaching.* New York: Cambridge University Press.

Minami, M., & Ovando, C. J. (2004). Language issues in multicultural contexts. In J. A. Banks & C. A. M. Banks (Eds.), *Handbook of research on multicultural education* (2nd ed., pp. 427–444). San Francisco: Jossey-Bass.

Miramontes, O. B., Nadeau, A., & Commins, N. L. (1997). *Restructuring schools for linguistic diversity.* New York: Teachers College Press.

Nieto, S. (2004). *Affirming diversity: The sociopolitical context for multicultural education* (4th ed.). White Plains, NY: Longman.

Ovando, C. J., Combs, M. C., & Collier, C. P. (2006). *Bilingual and ESL classrooms: Teaching in multicultural contexts* (4th ed.). New York: McGraw-Hill.

Snow, M. A. (2005b). Primary language instruction: A bridge to English language development. In California State Department of Education, *Schooling and language minority students: A theoretico-practical framework* (3rd ed., pp. 119–160). Los Angeles: California State University Evaluation, Dissemination, and Assessment Center.

Thomas, W. P., & Collier, V. P. (2002). *A national study of school effectiveness for language minority students' long-term academic achievement.* Santa Cruz: University of California Center for Research on Education, Diversity, and Excellence.

Collaboration

Hamayan, E., & Freeman, R. (Eds.). (2006). *English language learners at school: A guide for administrators.* Philadelphia: Caslon.

Pawan, F., & Sietman, G. B. (Eds.). (2007). *Helping English language learners succeed in middle and high schools.* Alexandria, VA: Teachers of English to Speakers of Other Languages.

Content-Based Instruction

Adamson, H. D. (1993). *Academic competence: Theory and classroom practice: Preparing ESL students for content courses.* New York: Longman.

Carr, J., Sexton, U., & Lagunoff, R. (2006). *Making science accessible to English learners.* San Francisco: WestEd.

Chamot, A. U., & O'Malley, J. M. (1994). *The CALLA handbook: Implementing the cognitive academic language learning approach.* New York: Addison-Wesley.

Coggins, D., Kravin, D., Coates, G. D., & Carroll, M. D. (2007). *English language learners in the mathematics classroom.* Thousand Oaks, CA: Corwin Press.

Echevarria, J., Short, D. J., & Vogt, M. E. (2008). *Making content comprehensible for English language learners: The SIOP model* (3rd ed.). Boston: Allyn & Bacon.

Ernst-Slavit, G., Moore, M., & Maloney, C. (2002). Changing lives: Teaching English and literature to ESL students. *Journal of Adolescent and Adult Literacy, 48*(2), 116–128.

Faltis, C. (1997). *Joinfostering: Adapting teaching for the multilingual classroom* (2nd ed.). Upper Saddle River, NJ: Merrill.

Fathman, A. K., & Crowther, D. T. (Eds.). (2006). *Science for English language learners: K–12 classroom strategies.* Arlington, VA: National Science Teachers Association Press.

Fordham, N., Wellman, D., & Sandman, A. (2002). Taming the text: Engaging and supporting students in social studies readings. *The Social Studies, 93*(4), 149–158.

Kaufman, D., & Crandall, J. (Eds.). (2005). *Content-based instruction in primary and secondary school settings.* Alexandria, VA: Teachers of English to Speakers of Other Languages.

Mohan, B. (1986). *Language and content.* Reading, MA: Addison-Wesley.

Reiss, J. (2001). *ESOL strategies for teaching content: Facilitating instruction for English language learners.* Upper Saddle River, NJ: Prentice-Hall.

Reiss, J. (2005). *Teaching content to English language learners.* White Plains, NY: Pearson Longman.

Richard-Amato, P. A. (2003). *Making it happen: From interactive to participatory language teaching* (3rd ed.). White Plains, NY: Pearson Education.

Settlage, J., & Southerland, S. A. (2007). *Teaching science to every child: Using culture as a starting point.* New York: Taylor & Francis.

Short, D. J. (1994a). The challenge of social studies for limited English proficient students. *Social Education, 58*(1), 36–38.

Short, D. J. (1994b). Expanding middle school horizons: Integrating language, culture, and social studies. *TESOL Quarterly, 28,* 581–608.

Short, D. J. (2002). Language and learning in sheltered social studies classes. *TESOL Journal, 11*(1), 18–24.

Snow, M. A., & Brinton, D. M. (Eds.). (1997). *The content-based classroom: Perspectives on integrating language and content.* White Plains, NY: Addison-Wesley.

Curriculum

Graves, K. (2000). *Designing language courses.* Boston: Heinle & Heinle.

Tomlinson, C. A., & McTighe, J. (2006). *Integrating differentiated instruction and understanding by design: Connecting content and kids.* Alexandria, VA: Association for Supervision and Curriculum Development.

English Language Learners With Special Needs

Baca, L. M., & Cervantes, H. T. (2004). *The bilingual special education interface* (4th ed.). Upper Saddle River, NJ: Pearson Education.

Genesee, F., Paradis, J., & Crago, M. B. (2004). *Dual language development and disorders: A handbook on bilingualism and second language learning.* Baltimore: Paul H. Brookes.

Hamayan, E., Marler, B., Sanchez-Lopez, C., & Damico, J. (2007). *Special education considerations for English language learners: Delivering a continuum of services.* Philadelphia: Caslon.

Literacy and Oral Language Development of English Language Learners

August, D., & Shanahan, T. (Eds.). (2006). *Developing literacy in second-language learners: Report of the national literacy panel on language-minority children and youth.* Mahwah, NJ: Lawrence Erlbaum.

Bauman, J. F., Kame'enui, E. J., & Ash, G. E. (2002). Research on vocabulary instruction: Voltaire redux. In J. Flood, D. Lapp, D. R. Squire, & J. Jensen (Eds.), *Handbook of research on the teaching of English language arts* (pp. 752–785). Mahwah, NJ: Lawrence Erlbaum.

Chen, L., & Mora-Flores, E. (2006). *Balanced literacy for English language learners, K–2.* Portsmouth, NH: Heinemann.

Christensen, L. (2000). *Reading, writing, and rising up.* Milwaukee, WI: Rethinking Schools.

Crabbe, D. (2003). The quality of language learning opportunities. *TESOL Quarterly, 37,* 9–34.

Dutro, S., & Moran, C. (2003). Rethinking English language instruction: An architectural approach. In G. Garcia (Ed.), *English learners: Reaching the highest level of English literacy* (pp. 227–258). Newark, DE: International Reading Association.

Enright, D. S., & McCloskey, M. L. (1988). *Integrating English: Developing English language and literacy in the multilingual classroom.* Reading, MA: Addison-Wesley.

Ernst, G. (1994). Talking circle: Conversation and negotiation in the ESL classroom. *TESOL Quarterly, 28,* 293–322.

Ernst-Slavit, G., & Mulhern, M. (2003, September/October). Bilingual books: Promoting literacy and biliteracy in the second-language and mainstream classroom. *Reading Online,* 7(2). Retrieved August 28, 2008, from http://www.readingonline.org/articles/art_index .asp?HREF=ernst-slavit/index.html

Freeman, Y. S., & Freeman, D. (2000). *Teaching reading in multicultural classrooms.* Portsmouth, NH: Heinemann.

Gibbons, P. (2002). *Scaffolding language, scaffolding learning.* Portsmouth, NH: Heinemann.

Goodman, K. S. (1992). *Language and literacy: The selected writings of Kenneth S. Goodman* (2 vols., F. V. Gollasch, Ed.). Boston: Routledge & Kegan Paul.

Green, J., & Dixon, C. (1993). Introduction: Talking knowledge into being: Discursive and social practices in classrooms. *Linguistics and Education, 5*(3&4), 231–239.

Hawkins, M. R. (2004). Researching English language and literacy development in schools. *Educational Researcher 33*(3), 14–25.

Hill, B. C. (2001). *Developmental continuums: A framework for literacy instruction and assessment K–8.* Norwood, MA: Christopher-Gordon.

Kucer, S. B. (2005). *Dimensions of literacy: A conceptual base for teaching reading and writing in school settings* (2nd ed.). Mahwah, NJ: Lawrence Erlbaum.

Kucer, S. B., & Silva, C. (2006). *Teaching the dimensions of literacy.* Mahwah, NJ: Lawrence Erlbaum.

McCarty, T. L. (Ed.). (2005). *Language, literacy, and power in schooling.* Mahwah, NJ: Lawrence Erlbaum.

Peregoy, S., & Boyle, O. (2005). *Reading, writing, and learning in ESL: A resource book for teachers* (4th ed.). Boston: Pearson.

Slavin, R. E., & Cheung, A. (2003). *Effective reading programs for English language learners: A best-evidence synthesis* (Report No. 66). Baltimore: Johns Hopkins University, Center for Research on the Education of Students Placed at Risk.

Slavin, R. E., & Cheung, A. (2004). How do English language learners learn to read? *Educational Leadership, 61*(6), 52–57.

Snow, M. A. (2005a). A model of academic literacy for integrated language and content instruction. In E. Hinkel (Ed.), *Handbook of research in second language teaching and learning* (pp. 693–712). Mahwah, NJ: Lawrence Erlbaum.

Tinajero, J. V., & Ada, A. F. (Eds.). (1993). *The power of two languages: Literacy and biliteracy for Spanish-speaking students.* New York: Macmillan/McGraw-Hill.

Vacca, R. T., & Vacca, J. L. (2007). *Content area reading: Literacy and learning across the curriculum* (9th ed.). Boston: Allyn & Bacon.

Standards-Based Education

Agor, B. (Ed.). (2001). *Integrating the ESL standards into classroom practice: Grades 9–12.* Alexandria, VA: Teachers of English to Speakers of Other Languages.

American Council for the Teaching of Foreign Languages. (1986). *ACTFL proficiency guidelines.* Hastings-on-Hudson, NY: Author.

American Educational Research Association & American Psychological Association. (1999). *Standards for educational and psychological testing.* Washington, DC: American Psychological Association.

Council of Europe. (2001). *Common European framework of reference for languages: Learning, teaching, assessment.* Cambridge: Cambridge University Press.

Drake, S. M. (2007). *Creating standards-based integrated curriculum: Aligning content, assessment, and instruction* (2nd ed.). Thousand Oaks, CA: Corwin Press.

Fisher, D., Rothenberg, C., & Frey, N. (2007). *Language learners in the English classroom.* Urbana, IL: National Council of Teachers of English.

Gottlieb, M. (2004). *WIDA Consortium English language proficiency standards for English language learners in kindergarten through grade 12: Overview document.* Madison: State of Wisconsin.

Irujo, S. (Ed.). (2001). *Integrating the ESL standards into classroom practice: Grades 6–8.* Alexandria, VA: Teachers of English to Speakers of Other Languages.

Kendall, J. S., & Marzano, R. J. (1997). *Content knowledge: A compendium of standards and benchmarks for K–12 education* (2nd ed.). Alexandria, VA: Association for Supervision and Curriculum Development.

Kuhlman, N., & Nadeau, A. (1999). English language development standards: The California model. *CATESOL Journal, 11*(1), 143–160.

McKeon, D. (1994). When meeting "common" standards is uncommonly difficult. *Educational Leadership, 51*(8), 45–49.

Morrow, K. (2004). *Insights from the Common European Framework.* Oxford: Oxford University Press.

Neill, M., Guisbond, L., & Schaeffer, B. (2004). *Failing our children: How "No Child Left Behind" undermines quality and equity in education: An accountability model that supports school improvement.* Cambridge, MA: FairTest.

Sacks, P. (1999). *Standardized minds: The high price of America's testing culture and what we can do to change it.* New York: Perseus Books.

Samway, K. D. (Ed.). (2001). *Integrating the ESL standards into classroom practice: Grades 3–5.* Alexandria, VA: Teachers of English to Speakers of Other Languages.

Short, D. J., Gómez, E. L., Cloud, N., Katz, A., Gottlieb, M., Malone, M. (with Hamayan, E., Hudelson, S., & Ramirez, J.). (2002). *Training others to use the ESL standards: A professional development manual.* Alexandria, VA: Teachers of English to Speakers of Other Languages.

Smallwood, B. A. (Ed.). (2001). *Integrating the ESL standards into classroom practice: Grades pre-K–2.* Alexandria, VA: Teachers of English to Speakers of Other Languages.

Snow, M. A. (Ed.). (2000). *Implementing the ESL standards for pre-K–12 students through teacher education.* Alexandria, VA: Teachers of English to Speakers of Other Languages.

Teachers of English to Speakers of Other Languages. (1997). *ESL standards for pre-K–12 students.* Alexandria, VA: Author.

Teachers of English to Speakers of Other Languages. (1998). *Managing the assessment process: A framework for measuring student attainment of the ESL standards* (TESOL Professional Papers No. 5). Alexandria, VA: Author.

Trumbull, E., & Farr, B. (Eds.). (2000). *Grading and reporting student progress in an age of standards.* Norwood, MA: Christopher-Gordon.

Appendixes

Appendix A
Content Topics Informing the TESOL English Language Proficiency Standards

(Reprinted from *PreK–12 English Language Proficiency Standards*
[TESOL, 2006, pp. 143–147].)

Standards-Based Language Functions and Topics (PreK–12; TESOL, 1997)

Goal 1: To use English to communicate in social settings	Goal 2: To use English to achieve academically in all content areas	Goal 3: To use English in socially and culturally appropriate ways
• Describe feelings and emotions • Defend and argue a position • Indicate interests, opinions, or preferences • Give and ask for permission • Offer and respond to greetings, compliments, invitations, introductions, and farewells • Negotiate solutions to problems, interpersonal misunderstandings, and disputes • Clarify and restate information • Write personal essays • Describe favorite storybook characters • Recount events of interest • Make recommendations • Use the primary language to ask for clarification • Associate realia or diagrams with written labels • Use written sources to discover or check information • Share social and cultural traditions and values • Use context to construct meaning • Self-monitor and self-evaluate language development	• Compare and classify information • Synthesize, analyze, and evaluate information • Research information from multiple sources • Take a position and support it • Construct a chart • Identify and associate written symbols with words • Define, compare, and classify objects • Locate information • Edit and revise own written assignments • Use contextual clues • Consult print and nonprint resources in the native language • Write a summary • Record observations • Skim and scan materials • Rephrase, explain, revise, and expand information • Follow directions • Ask and answer questions • Express likes, dislikes, and needs • Explain actions • Gather and retell information • Represent information visually and interpret information presented visually • Connect new information to information previously learned	• Recognize irony, sarcasm, and humor • Use idiomatic speech • Write business and personal letters • Write letters or e-mail messages using appropriate language forms • Compare body language norms among various cultures • Identify nonverbal cues that cause misunderstanding • Rephrase an utterance when it results in cultural misunderstanding • Respond to and use slang and idioms

Topics Drawn From National and State Academic Content Standards

Grade-Level Cluster	Academic Content Area			
	Language Arts and Reading	Mathematics	Science	Social Studies
PreK–K	**Genres** • Nursery rhymes • Chants and songs • Picture books • Fairy tales **Topics** • Environmental print • Concepts about print • Sounds and symbols	• Quantity • Patterns • Size • Spatial relations • Geometric shapes • Weight • Temperature • Measurement of time (calendar, clocks) • Numbers and operations	• Senses • Living things • Change in self and environment • Forces in nature • Seasons, night and day • Weather • Safety • Animals and habitats • Scientific process • Colors	• Community workers • Families • Location of objects and places • Transportation • Clothing • Food • Shelter • Holidays and symbols • Classroom, school • Neighborhood • Friends
1–3	**Genres** • Fiction • Nonfiction • Poetry • Predictable books • Folktales **Topics** • Sequence of story • Word families • Rhyming words • Homophones • Compound words • Story grammar • Phonics and phonemic awareness	• Time (digital and analog) • Measurement tools (standard, nonstandard, metric) • Place value • Money • Estimation • Capacity • Symmetry • Basic operations (addition and subtraction) • Whole numbers	• Light • Motion • Weathering and erosion • Renewable and nonrenewable resources • Plants • Animals • Life cycles • Living and nonliving things • Sound • Objects in the sky • Organisms and environment • Astronomy • Water cycle	• Needs of groups, societies, and cultures • Artifacts of the past • Representations of the earth (maps, globes, and photographs) • Land forms • Scale • Use of resources and land • Citizenship • Communities • Governments • Cultural heritage • Time and chronology

Grade-Level Cluster	Academic Content Area			
	Language Arts and Reading	**Mathematics**	**Science**	**Social Studies**
4–5	**Genres** • Biographies and autobiography • Fables • Fairy tales • Fantasy • Folklore • Informational texts • Legends • Mysteries • Myths • Narratives • Prose • Science fiction • Tall tales **Topics** • Affixes and root words • Fact and opinion • Hyperbole • Main ideas and details • Organization of texts • Phonemes and phonology • Point of view • Story grammar • Text structure and organization	• Angles • Area • Basic operations (multiplication and division) • Decimals • Descriptive statistics • Equivalent forms (fractions, decimals, and percent) • Fractions • Patterns and relationships • Percent • Perimeter • Polygons • Sets • Three-dimensional shapes • Data analysis • Patterns, relations, and functions	• Cells and organisms • Earth materials • Ecology and conservation • Ecosystems • Electricity • Energy sources • Forces of nature • Fossils • Geological forms • Heat • Magnetism • Reproduction and heredity • Scientific inquiry • Simple machines • Solar system • States of matter • Weather patterns • Types of resources • Body systems • Natural resources • Earth's history • Living systems	• Branches of government • Colonization • Communities • Explorers • Goods and services • Historical events, figures, and leaders • Immigration • Legends and scales • Maps and globes • Neighbors north and south • Prehistoric animals • Resources and products • Tools and artifacts • Topography • Trade routes • U.S. documents • U.S. regions: Rivers, coasts, mountains, deserts, and plains • Cross-cultural experiences

Grade-Level Cluster	Academic Content Area			
	Language Arts and Reading	Mathematics	Science	Social Studies
6–8	**Genres** • Adventure • Ballads • Editorials • Historical documents • Human interest • Multimedia • Mythology • Poetry and free verse • Science fiction • Technical texts **Topics** • Alliteration • Author's purpose • Dialogue • Metaphors and similes • Multiple meanings • Personification • Synonyms, antonyms, and homophones • Use of resources (including strategies and editing)	• Area, volume, and circumference • Complex two- and three-dimensional figures • Data sets and plots • Factors • Integers • Interpreting data and statistics • Line segments and angles • Measures of central tendency • Metric and U.S. customary units of measurement • Probability • Ratio and proportion • Square root • Statistics	• Atoms and molecules • Bacteria to plants • Body systems and organs • Chemical building blocks • Climate zones • Comets and meteorites • Elements and compounds • Forms of energy • Light • Motion and force • Natural disasters • Reproduction • Scientific invention • Solar system • Temperature changes • Water • Populations, resources, and environments	• Ancient and medieval civilizations • Bill of Rights • Civil War • Countries and continents • Forms and organization of government • Freedom and democracy • Longitude, latitude, and time zones • Revolution • Rights and responsibilities • Slavery • U.S. Constitution • Cultural perspectives and frames of reference

Grade-Level Cluster	Academic Content Area			
	Language Arts and Reading	Mathematics	Science	Social Studies
9–12	**Genres** • Critical commentary • Literary genres • Monologues • Research and investigation • Autobiographical and biographical narratives **Topics** • Analogies • Author's perspective and point of view • Bias • Parody • Satire • Symbolism • Word derivations (etymology) • Literal and figurative language	• Data displays and interpretation • Derived attributes • Formulas and equations • Mathematical functions • Powers • Roots • Speed and acceleration • Angles • Quadrilaterals • Models • Scale and proportion • Congruence	• Atoms, molecules, and nuclear structures • Chemical and physical change • Compounds • Constellations • Food chains • Forces and motion • Genetics and heredity • Scientific research and investigation • Simple organisms • Taxonomic systems • Vertebrates and invertebrates • Conservation of energy and matter • Classification • Ecology and adaptation	• Global economy • Historical figures and times • Individual rights and responsibilities • Social issues and inequities • The story of the United States • World histories, civilizations, and cultures • Cultural diversity and cohesion • International and multinational organizations • Supreme Court cases • Federal, civil, and individual rights • Behaviors of individuals and groups • Production, consumption, and distribution • Supply and demand • Banking and money • Human populations

Appendix B
A Blank English Language Proficiency Standards Matrix

Standard: _____   Grade-Level Cluster: _____

Domain	Topic	Level 1	Level 2	Level 3	Level 4	Level 5

NATIVE LANGUAGES & CULTURES

This blank standards matrix may be used in pre-service settings, to acclimate potential teachers to the developmental progression of language acquisition within the context of a specific language domain and topic, or in in-service settings, as part of professional development on standards-based education of English language learners.

Appendix C
Planning Professional Development
Using the PreK–12 English Language Proficiency Standards

A Standards-Based Professional Development Plan

Workshop/Course Topic	Description or Objectives of Workshop/Course	Participants, Dates, and Duration (in hours or days)

Paper to Practice: Using the TESOL English Language Proficiency Standards in PreK–12 Classrooms

Appendix D
Transforming Elements of
Sample Performance Indicators

Grade-level cluster: _____

Standard: _____

Language domain: _____

Topic: _____

Level of English language proficiency: _____

Transform the Language Function

A.

Transform the Topic or Content

B.

Transform the Support

C.

Appendix E
A Template for Developing Strands of Sample Performance Indicators

Standard: _____

Grade Level: _____

Language Domain(s): _____

Topic	Level 1	Level 2	Level 3	Level 4	Level 5

Appendix F
Sample Home Language Survey
for New Students

This survey should be completed by the student's parent or guardian upon school enrollment.

1. Which language did your child learn when first beginning to talk? _____

2. Which language does **your child** use most frequently at home? _____

3. Which language do **you** normally use when speaking to your child? _____

4. Which language do the **adults** in the home speak most often? _____

5. Was your child born in the United States?   yes ☐   no ☐

   If not, when did your child come to the United States?   year: _____

6. Put an **X** in the boxes on the top line to show the grades your child has gone to school in the United States. Put an **X** in the boxes on the bottom line to show the grades your child went to school in another country.

School	Grade														
Schools **in** the United States	PreK	K	1	2	3	4	5	6	7	8	9	10	11	12
Schools **outside** of the United States	PreK	K	1	2	3	4	5	6	7	8	9	10	11	12

7. If your child has gone to school **outside** the United States:

   In which country or countries did your child go to school? _____

   Which language or languages did your child learn in school? _____

Appendix G
Sample Literacy Survey for
English Language Learners

(Adapted from Gottlieb, 2006, p. 18.)

What can you read? In each row, mark the box with an **X** to show if you use your first language, English, or both languages to read this item. Mark the last box with an **X** if you do not read this item at all.

I CAN READ . . .	In my first language	In English	In both languages	Not at all
1. Signs				
2. Maps				
3. Schedules (e.g., school, bus, or train)				
4. Text messages				
5. Newspapers				
6. Magazines				
7. Notes from friends				
8. Information from the Internet				
9. Brochures, pamphlets, or newsletters				
10. Short stories				
11. Poetry				
12. Books				

Paper to Practice: Using the TESOL English Language Proficiency Standards in PreK–12 Classrooms

What can you write? In each row, mark the box with an **X** to show if you use your first language, English, or both languages to write this item. Mark the last box with an **X** if you do not write this item at all.

I CAN WRITE . . .	In my first language	In English	In both languages	Not at all
1. Words that go with pictures or charts				
2. Information on forms				
3. Lists				
4. Memos or notes				
5. E-mails				
6. Letters				
7. Stories				
8. Poetry				
9. Reports				

Appendix H
Guide for Unit Planning

Step From the Language Curriculum Framework	What I Do
Previewing: What is the context for language instruction?	
Step 1: Determine English language learners' current language profiles.	
Step 2: Analyze the language demands of the content topic.	
Planning: How is language incorporated into lesson design?	
Step 3: Match ELP standards to language demands, and decide whether and which transformations are necessary.	
Step 4: Develop language objectives.	
Step 5: Differentiate instructional activities according to levels of language proficiency.	
Step 6: Plan for instructional supports.	
Reflecting: Is language learning taking place? How do we know?	
Step 7: Review evidence of language learning and decide next steps.	

Paper to Practice: Using the TESOL English Language Proficiency Standards in PreK–12 Classrooms

Appendix I
A Standards-Based Language
Curriculum Framework Checklist

Lesson/Unit: _____

Grade level(s): _____   Date: _____

☑ Check off each step as you complete it.

PREVIEWING

Step 1: Determine English language learners' current language profiles.

☐ Complete the English Language Learners' Profile Form (see Appendix J).

☐ Become familiar with the performance definitions of the five levels of English language proficiency in Figure 3.1 of this book or on page 39 of *PreK–12 English Language Proficiency Standards* (TESOL, 2006).

Step 2: Analyze the language demands of the content topic.

☐ List *vocabulary* (words, phrases and expressions) from your lesson/unit that students need to know. Include

    ○ everyday vocabulary

    ○ instructional vocabulary

    ○ academic vocabulary

☐ List *grammatical structures* used in your lesson/unit.

☐ List *discourse forms* present in your lesson/unit.

PLANNING

Step 3: Match ELP standards to language demands, and decide whether and which transformations are necessary.

☐ Complete the box based on your lesson/unit goals.

Standard _____: _____

Topic: _____

Grade-level cluster: ☐ preK–K ☐ 1–3 ☐ 4–5 ☐ 6–8 ☐ 9–12

Language domain: ☐ listening ☐ speaking ☐ reading ☐ writing

☐ Locate the sample performance indicators (SPIs) in *PreK–12 English Language Proficiency Standards* (TESOL, 2006) that correspond with your grade level and content area.

☐ Compare the SPIs to your lesson/unit plan.

☐ Complete the box to show which elements of the SPIs need to be changed:

Language domain(s): ☐ No change needed. ☐ Change to _____.

Topic: ☐ No change needed. ☐ Change to match my content.

Language functions: ☐ No change needed. ☐ Change to _____.

Instructional supports: ☐ No change needed. ☐ Change to _____.

Step 4: Develop language objectives.

☐ Students at Level 1:

_____

_____

_____

☐ Students at Level 2:

_____

_____

_____

☐ Students at Level 3:

_____

_____

_____

☐ Students at Level 4:

_____

_____

_____

☐ Students at Level 5:

_____

_____

_____

Step 5: Differentiate instructional activities according to levels of language proficiency.

☐ Review the performance definitions of the five levels of English language proficiency in Figure 3.1.

☐ Using these performance definitions as a guide, begin to craft differentiated activities based on appropriate language expectations.

☐ Complete the chart, listing specific examples of

   ○ vocabulary words and phrases

   ○ language functions

   ○ grammatical structures

   ○ discourse forms

Language Targets	Level 1: _____	Level 2: _____	Level 3: _____	Level 4: _____	Level 5+ (All Other Students)
Vocabulary					
Language Functions					
Grammar					
Discourse					

Paper to Practice: Using the TESOL English Language Proficiency Standards in PreK–12 Classrooms

☐ Check your chart to make sure that

    ◯ the number of required vocabulary words and phrases is reasonable (You can negotiate this with your English language learners.)

    ◯ the number of words and phrases is differentiated by ELP level

☐ Consider possible strategies, activities, and structures that might benefit different students.

☐ Consider possible products—that is, what students will do to show that they have learned the content.

Step 6: Plan for instructional supports.

☐ Brainstorm a list of possible supports that would be appropriate to your subject matter, the age of your students, and the resources you have available. Refer to Figure 4.9 for ideas.

☐ Remember to include the ELL instructional assistant or paraprofessional, if available, as one source of support.

Level 1	Level 2	Level 3	Level 4	Level 5

REFLECTING

Step 7: Review evidence of language learning and decide next steps.

☐ Did you consider evidence for both receptive and productive language?

☐ Did you adapt and/or differentiate assessment expectations?

☐ Did you complete a Teacher to ELL Paraprofessional Planning and Instruction Sheet, if appropriate? (See Appendix L.)

☐ Other notes: _____

_____

_____

_____

_____

_____

_____

_____

_____

_____

_____

_____

_____

_____

_____

_____

_____

_____

Appendix J
English Language Learners' Profile Form

English Language Learner	Most Recent Test Scores (ELP Level)						Country of Origin and Native Language	Personal Characteristics
		1	2	3	4	5		
	L							
	S							
	R							
	W							
	L							
	S							
	R							
	W							
	L							
	S							
	R							
	W							
	L							
	S							
	R							
	W							

Appendix K
Original Mathematics Lesson Plan

Unit: Who Are We?

Lesson 1. Our Names: Valuable Vowels

Learning Objectives

Students will

- collect and classify data
- create a bar graph
- compare and contrast bar graphs
- ask and answer questions about a data set
- calculate the range and mode of a data set

Materials

- ☐ markers, pens, or crayons
- ☐ index cards
- ☐ tape
- ☐ grid paper
- ☐ computer with graphing program or Internet access
- ☐ projector and screen
- ☐ chalkboard, whiteboard, or butcher paper

Instructional Plan

Building Background / Assessing Prior Knowledge:

Display a bar graph from a book, newspaper, or other source. Ask students questions about the graph in order to assess and review knowledge of data points, axes, and so on.

Activity:

1. Distribute index cards and give the following step-by-step instructions:

   - Ask students to write two things on their index cards: (1) their first name, and (2) the number of vowels in that name.

   - Instruct students to arrange themselves in groups according to the number of vowels in their first names. (While students are organizing themselves, write the numbers 1 through the highest number of vowels represented in your classroom vertically on the board or on butcher paper.)

   - Tell the students in each group to tape their index cards together horizontally, end-to-end, to form a long bar.

   - Ask students to tape their bars to the board or butcher paper next to the number representing the number of vowels in their names (see Figure K1).

   - At the right side of each row, write down how many names are in each group.

   - Poll students for possible names for this bar graph.

2. Distribute grid paper. Ask students to copy the bar graph onto their paper.

3. Ask students to explain what they can tell about the data by looking at their bar graphs. If students do not mention which numbers of vowels have the longest and shortest bars, guide them to this understanding.

4. Tell students that the value with the longest bar is called the *mode*. (In Figure K1, the mode is 2.) When two values are tied for the longest bar, the data are called *bimodal*. Explain that the *mode* is one way to measure central tendency.

1	Kim				1
2	Joe	Sue	Luis	Steve	4
3	Celeste	Ramona			2
4	Alexandra	Antonio	Catherine		3

Figure K1. Sample Bar Graph Using Index Cards.

5. Ask students to calculate the *range* of the data by subtracting the lowest number from the highest number. (In Figure K1, this would be 4 – 1, or 3.) Refer to this as the *measure of spread*.

6. Open a computer graphing program. Display it for the whole class, using a projector or other means.

7. Ask student volunteers to enter the class data into the program. Ask students to type names for the values, the number of each value, and the title of the graph. In addition, ask volunteers to select a color for each bar.

8. Using the data now entered into the computer, create a horizontal bar graph (see Figure K2). Print the graph for future reference.

9. Return to the data entered and generate a vertical bar graph (see Figure K3). Print this graph for easy reference.

10. Ask students to compare and contrast the two graphs. Help students to see that the change in orientation of the bars does not affect the data.

11. Tell students to label and record the mode and the range of the data set.

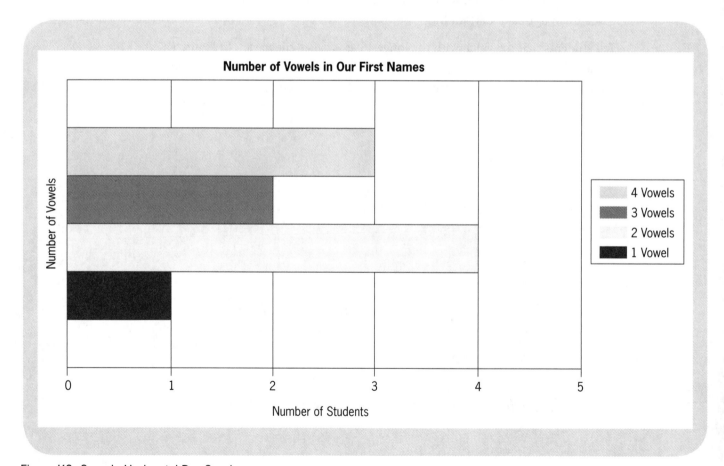

Figure K2. Sample Horizontal Bar Graph.

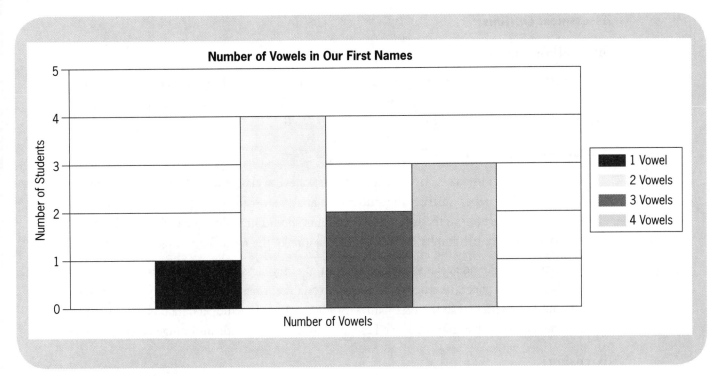

Figure K3. Sample Vertical Bar Graph.

Questions for Students

1. How many students had

   - one vowel in their name?

   - two vowels in their names?

   - three vowels in their names? (etc.)

2. How many vowels were in the

   - largest number of names?

   - smallest number of names?

   How do you know?

3. What word do we use to describe the difference between the largest and the smallest number? (range) What is the range of the data we collected?

4. What is different about the horizontal and vertical bar graphs? What is the same?

5. Imagine that (name a student with 2 vowels in his/her first name) left the class. How would the bar graph change? What would happen to the mode?

6. What would happen to the range if I added my name to the list? What would happen to the mode? What would the bar graph look like?

Assessment Options

Informal Assessment:

Make a class list with space for notes about each student. While walking around the classroom, take note of students' progress. Write brief notes on your list, make checkmarks, or use a coded system to indicate progress quickly.

Formal Assessment:

1. *More Vowels:* Provide each student with a list of every classmate's last name and a new sheet of grid paper. Instruct the students to analyze, organize, and display data on the vowels present in the last names. Students should include a data table and both orientations of bar graphs, as well as calculations of the mode and range of the data set.

2. *Consonants:* Provide each student with a list of every classmate's first name and a new sheet of grid paper. Instruct the students to analyze, organize, and display data on the consonants present in the first names. Students should include a data table and both orientations of bar graphs, as well as calculations of the mode and range of the data set.

Extension

Ask students to express the number of vowels in their first names using a fraction. Repeat with consonants. For example, in *Michael* $^3/_7$ of the letters are vowels and $^4/_7$ of the letters are consonants.

Teacher Reflection

1. Which students met the lesson objectives? Which did not?

2. What worked well? What should/could I do differently next time?

Resources for the Teacher

Online graphing tools can be found at the following Web sites:

National Center for Education Statistics (NCES)
  http://nces.ed.gov/nceskids/createagraph/

National Council of Teachers of Mathematics (NCTM)
  http://illuminations.nctm.org/ActivityDetail.aspx?ID=63

MotionNet
  http://graphtools.com/

Appendix L
Teacher to ELL Paraprofessional
Planning and Instruction Sheet

Name of ELL Paraprofessional: _____

Name of Teacher and Grade Level: _____

Name(s) of English Language Learners: _____

Tasks and Goals

Time Frame: _____

TESOL Standard:

1. Social/Instructional   2. Language Arts   3. Math   4. Science   5. Social Studies

Topic: _____

Content Objectives: _____

Language Objectives: _____

Instructional Supports Needed: _____

Materials Needed: _____

Location of Materials and Supports: _____

Procedures: _____

_____

_____

_____

_____

Comments from ELL Paraprofessional: _____

_____

_____

_____

Appendix M
Watershed Ecosystems Project Rubric:
Multimedia Report

Student: _____   Date: _____

Language Proficiency Level 5

☐ I analyze, review, and critique the steps of scientific inquiry.

☐ I discuss causes and effects of pollution on water samples based on my hypotheses.

☐ I use pictures or diagrams to support my ideas.

☐ I use complex sentences with specialized and technical language of science.

Language Proficiency Level 4

☐ I interpret information from the steps of scientific inquiry using a graph or chart.

☐ I state the probable causes and effects of pollution on water samples based on my hypotheses.

☐ I use pictures or diagrams to explain and give examples of my ideas.

☐ I use a variety of sentences with specialized science words.

Language Proficiency Level 3

☐ I order the steps of scientific inquiry using a graph or chart and sequential language.

☐ I say what I think will happen and what does happen to the water samples based on my hypotheses.

☐ I use pictures or diagrams to describe my ideas in detail.

☐ I connect sentences using general and specialized science words.

Language Proficiency Level 2

- [ ] I describe the steps of scientific inquiry using a T-chart.

- [ ] I compare water samples in stating my hypotheses.

- [ ] I use pictures or diagrams to state my ideas.

- [ ] I use general science words in sentences.

Language Proficiency Level 1

- [ ] I show the steps of the experiment with pictures.

- [ ] I tell what I think will happen to the water samples.

- [ ] I use pictures or diagrams to express my ideas

- [ ] I use general science words and phrases.

Appendix N
Watershed Ecosystems Project Rubric: Letter of Recommendation

Student: _____   Date: _____

Language Proficiency Level 5

☐ I suggest a course of action backed by summary data on water quality in the watershed.

☐ My writing has fully developed paragraphs in business letter form.

☐ My letter has concise information that analyzes the results of our scientific inquiry.

☐ My letter is persuasive yet uses language respectful to public officials.

Language Proficiency Level 4

☐ I make recommendations to public officials based on data about water quality in the watershed.

☐ My letter has related sentences in paragraph form.

☐ My letter has relevant information that summarizes the process and results of our scientific inquiry.

☐ My letter explains my point of view, with language appropriate for use with public officials.

Language Proficiency Level 3

☐ I describe the water quality in the watershed based on data and ask questions about the results to public officials.

☐ My letter has complete sentences and a salutation, body, and closing.

☐ My letter describes the process and results of our scientific inquiry.

☐ My letter states my ideas, with language appropriate for use with adults.

Also Available From TESOL

CALL Environments: Research, Practice, and Critical Issues, 2nd ed.
Joy Egbert and E. Hanson-Smith, Editors

Content-Based Instruction in Primary and Secondary School Settings
Dorit Kaufman and JoAnn Crandall, Editors

Developing a New Curriculum for Adult Learners
Michael Carroll, Editor

ESOL Tests and Testing
Stephen Stoynoff and Carol A. Chapelle

Helping English Language Learners Succeed in Pre-K–12 Elementary Schools
Jan Lacina, Linda New Levine, and Patience Sowa

Helping English Language Learners Succeed in Middle and High Schools
F. Pawan and G. Sietman, Editors

Learning Languages through Technology
Elizabeth Hanson-Smith and Sarah Rilling, Editors

Language Teacher Research in Asia
Thomas S. C. Farrell, Editor

Language Teacher Research in Europe
Simon Borg, Editor

Language Teacher Research in the Americas
Hedy McGarrell, Editor

Language Teacher Research in the Middle East
Christine Coombe and Lisa Barlow, Editors

Language Teacher Research in Australia and New Zealand
Jill Burton and Anne Burns, Editors

Literature in Language Teaching and Learning
Amos Paran, Editor

More Than a Native Speaker: An Introduction to Teaching English Abroad
revised edition
Don Snow

Perspectives on Community College ESL Series
Craig Machado, Series Editor
Volume 1: Pedagogy, Programs, Curricula, and Assessment
Marilynn Spaventa, Editor
Volume 2: Students, Mission, and Advocacy
Amy Blumenthal, Editor
Volume 3: Faculty, Administration, and the Working Environment
Jose A.Carmona, Editor

PreK–12 English Language Proficiency Standards
Teachers of English to Speakers of Other Languages, Inc.

Planning and Teaching Creatively within a Required Curriculum for School-Age Learners
Penny McKay, Editor

Professional Development of International Teaching Assistants
Dorit Kaufman and Barbara Brownworth, Editors

Revitalizing an Established Program for Adult Learners
Alison Rice, Editor

Teaching English as a Foreign Language in Primary School
Mary Lou McCloskey, Janet Orr, and Marlene Dolitsky, Editors

To order TESOL books:

Local phone: (240)646-7037
Toll-free: 1-888-891-0041
Fax: (301)206-9789
E-Mail: tesolpubs@brightkey.net
Mail Orders to TESOL, P.O. Box 79283, Baltimore, MD 21279-0283 USA

ORDER ONLINE at www.tesol.org and click on "Bookstore"